The Simple Truth

D1400655

The Simple Truth

✦

Why Most Marriages Fail and How You Can Save Yours

Ed Smith

iUniverse, Inc.
New York Lincoln Shanghai

The Simple Truth
Why Most Marriages Fail and How You Can Save Yours

Copyright © 2006 by Edward L. Smith

All rights reserved. No part of this book may be used or reproduced by any means, graphic, electronic, or mechanical, including photocopying, recording, taping or by any information storage retrieval system without the written permission of the publisher except in the case of brief quotations embodied in critical articles and reviews.

iUniverse books may be ordered through booksellers or by contacting:

iUniverse
2021 Pine Lake Road, Suite 100
Lincoln, NE 68512
www.iuniverse.com
1-800-Authors (1-800-288-4677)

ISBN-13: 978-0-595-39941-3 (pbk)
ISBN-13: 978-0-595-84330-5 (ebk)
ISBN-10: 0-595-39941-X (pbk)
ISBN-10: 0-595-84330-1 (ebk)

Printed in the United States of America

Contents

General

If you enjoy reading this book, you just may be interested in other books written by Ed Smith, the author. Enumerated below is a list of some of his pervious writings and how each one of them may be purchased.

1. **I Never, Ever Spank/Beat my kids and they turned out okay.**
How to purchase—this book may be purchased via amazon.com or through publishamerica.com

2. **The D.C. Department of Corrections, as I saw it.**
How to purchase—go to Lulu.com at the top of the page next to the word SEARCH, type in the title of the book and click enter

3. **Dirty Old Men Making Babies, there ought to be a law.**
How to purchase—same as # 2, however, you may have to type in the author's name as being Edward Smith.

4. **Stop Lying In The Name Of God**
How to purchase—go to authorhouse.com at the top of the page, click on the words bookstore—or call 1-800-839-8640. This book may also be purchased through amazon.com

In reading this book you may ask yourself who is the author and what gives him the authority to write on such a sensitive subject. While the author has no degrees in the subject matter nor any other accolades that would certify him to be a so-called expert, he does possess more than thirty-two (32) of experience in the subject matter. As such, in his mind that qualifies him to be an expert. He is just an everyday average guy who cares about you, your marriage, your children and the condition of the world.

The author recognizes the critical state of marriages in this country and felt compelled to lend his voice in hopes of strengthen them. The author at one point, let me restart that sentence, he will not lie. The author on many occasions thought about getting a divorce. It was usually subsequent to an argument with his spouse.

Like so many of us in today's society whenever we are confronted with a problem we often times think it is much easier to run away before we even examine the consequences of our actions. The most important thing that kept the author centered is the fact that he had young children and he was more concerned about their future well being rather than his own personal needs. He also knew that if he had a problem he was better served by solving it rather than running. He used that very same logic in rasing his children.

The author clearly recognized the fact that even if he fled his marriage for the arms of another he would surely encounter problems with the other person. That is just the way it is in life. He knew that only he held the key to his eventual happiness. He therefore reasoned that it was far better to deal with his present situation. Again, he must be honest. He also reasoned that it would be a whole lot cheaper and time has proven him to be right in that regard.

The author recognized early in life that if he continued to breathe he would someday become a senior citizen and he would need someone to grow old with. He knew that while one is young he/she has no such thoughts. As he said earlier, time has qualified him to be an expert and he will clearly tell you that only a very few in our society really cares about senior citizens. He reasons that it would therefore behoove one to put aside his/her disagreements and attempt to cultivate a lasting union.

The author is not an English professor and while reading you may encounter some grammatical and punctuation errors. The author ask that you look beyond those errors and absorb the message. The author wishes that we could all be grammatically correct all the time in our language usage. If you the reader fails to read this book because of an error just remember that there are many more out there like the author who may make an error or two in writing. The book is about having a successful marriage.

Since for the most part there are more common people than professors, the author felt that he must speak to the masses in the most simple way and the best way he knows how. That may be a big part of the problem, we may have too many professors and professionals attempting to give us advise on everyday down to earth matters. They sometimes cannot clearly see the overall picture because their thoughts are based on statistical data.

The author guarantees that if you can't identify with some of the things being said in this book he will gladly refund your money. To him it isn't about the money but rather about this nation continued existence for his children and grandchildren and all the other people of the world. That my friend starts and stops with marriage and our children. If this country is to endure we must have strong unions which will generate balanced children.

The author feels that if he is going off to war he wants to go with someone who has been in the trenches rather than someone holding a book and telling him how it should be. Well, given the number of years that the author has been in the marriage trenches, he has clearly seen and encountered some of the pitfalls relative to the demise of a marriage and it is his sincere hope that this writing will cause you to take a closer look at yours in an attempt to improve it. He will share with you ways in which you can relieve some of the **stress** associated with marriage. How to agree to disagree. How to accept rather than reject.

You may come to conclude that the author is too judgmental and harsh. Common sense should compel one to conclude that if something isn't working it would behoove one to change courses. If someone tells me that I am more than fifty percent wrong about a subject matter and I want to improve my percentage points, it would behoove me to work on my negatives. Therefore, you may find a great deal of negatives in this book. They are only intended to get you to improve on them.

Inasmuch as more than fifty percent (50%) of the marriage in this country will fail we as a nation must stand up and acknowledge the fact that we have a serious problem that must be corrected. Adults in this country must set the example for our children. If two adults can't resolve their problems how can we expect our children to deal with rather than run from problems.

Should the fact that well over fifty percent (50%) of the marriages in this country will fail be alarming? Well it shouldn't be because for the most part we are trying to live up to some unreal and very unreasonable standards and expectations.

Let us be for real here, do you really and truly believe that you or any other human being on this earth can remain absolutely committed to another for the rest of their lives, when in fact it is most difficult enough to be totally committed to the goals we set for ourselves? Well, if you believe that one can be totally committed to another until death do them part, then I have a parcel of land that I want to sell you where the White House sits. I will sell you the land at a very good price.

When I talk about being committed I am not necessarily talking about cheating or any other form of infidelity. To clearly illustrate my point, I want you to take this little test and you will clearly be able to identify with what I am talking about. Go to the mirror and scrutinize yourself to the fullest. While examining yourself, realize that the mirror will only reveal the physical side of you.

Nonetheless, allow yourself to examine the inner-depth ness of your very soul. For example, how many times did you commit yourself to stop smoking? How many times did you commit yourself to start an exercise regime? How many times did you commit yourself to not eating so much? etc. etc.

While standing before the mirror, did you detect a roll of fat or some other situation that you may deem to be inappropriate? If you did detect any setback to your health that you are responsible for, what make you think that you can avoid setbacks with someone else.

How can you be totally committed to another person when it is difficult enough to be totally committed to maintaining a healthy weight? What makes you truly think that you can be totally committed to someone else when in fact, you couldn't even remain committed enough to yourself to put down all of that cake and other fattening foods over the years. How many unwanted pounds have you gained recently?

Commitment

The first and most important thing in life is to realize and recognize the fact that no matter how long you may live on this earth, you can never ever become as one with another human being because each and every one of us are bound by our own selfish idiosyncrasies. Although we may make an attempt to go beyond our limits to please someone else, the **stress** involved in such an endeavor will surely and certainly begin to take a toll on the person and the relationship. You will arrive at a point wherein you can no longer pretend to be happy trying to totally please others.

Over the years, I have learned that the human being is one of the most selfish animals created by our creator. For the most part, we want everything to be conducive to our own personal well being. When we so-call commit ourselves to all of those absurd wedding vows, what we are really saying is, I really hope this person can encourage me to live in the manner that I should and stop me from doing all of those wrong things that I am accustomed to doing.

For example, in order for me to reduce the risk of contracting any STDs, it would behoove me to stop being with so many different partners and settle down. In order for me to reduce my tax obligation, it would behoove me to get a spouse. In order for me to have more money in society, it would behoove me to get a spouse who is gainfully employed.

In order for me to have someone to blame for all of my shortcomings, it would behoove me to get a spouse. In order for me to convince others that I am family orientated, it would behoove me to have a spouse. If I am gay and I want to conceal that fact, it would behoove me to acquire an opposite sex partner. If I hurt others in the pursuit of reaching my desired objective, so be it. For I must look out for number one.

Although I know that I am a flawed human being, I cannot let the world know about this. If I am married, I will always have someone else to blame for my mistakes. Unfortunately, for the most part both married people feel the same way. Have you ever seen a married couple argue about a particular subject, no matter how big or small the issue it is always the other partner's fault and neither will give an inch.

It makes me wonder if people only marry just to validate their own personal beliefs. They knew that they couldn't really control their own personal behavior so they needed a personal sounding board to comfirm or validate themselves.

If we were totally honest and sincere with ourselves, we would commit ourselves to allow each other to be ourselves. In order to make any commitment achievable it must be reasonable. In order to have any possibility of accomplishing that task wedding vows should only consist of a few basic desires.

Number one and most important thy should not commit adultery. As you continue reading, I will clearly show you how you can overcome all the other issues that can ruin a marriage. Although some marriages thrive after an incident of adultery, it is the most difficult issue to overcome.

Whenever I think of or hear the word commitment relative to a marriage situation I think of a scenario wherein I will totally dedicate myself in the pursuit of making another human being happy for the rest of their life. Inasmuch as I couldn't keep a commitment to myself to stay away from all the wrong foods, is it reasonable and prudent for me to think that I can keep a commitment of that magnitude to someone else.

I know that I love myself, yet, where did all of these extra unhealthy pounds come from? Did someone put a loaded gun to my head and force me to overeat all of those times? No they didn't, it was my own personal inability to remain totally committed to myself.

First of all, I will venture and say that for the most part no one loves someone else more than they love themselves. Unless the couple has been married for a great number of years and they have learned to depend totally on the other. That is about the nearest a couple will become as being one and they only become that way out of habit from being around each other for so long. Another example may be a parent loving their children. I really can't think of too many young folks loving others more than themselves, because they think that they are God's gift to the world and the world just may stop if they are not in it.

Far too many young folks for the most part, seem to feel or think that life and the world is all about them and others are in it to ensure all of their comforts are satisfied. I say that because I was young once. Although they may pretend to love their children, the fact that they would obtain a divorce quickly disspells that thought.

Commitments, lets just examine a few. After a few years have passed in some marriages and both parties come to the realization that the utopia that they expected isn't really there, they become miserable. Now I know that you have heard the phrase that misery loves company. Believe me when I tell you, it is true.

In a case like this, one or both parties becomes committed to making the other's life a living hell. They must have someone to blame for getting them into this awful mess. Each of them will say things like I don't know why I married you in the first place.

All of my friends and family warned me that you were worthless, I wish that I had listened. When the couple reaches this point they have come to the realization that marriage is not the upotia they thought it would be and they now realize that they can't change the other into the model partner that they envisioned. Each will blame the other for wasting all that time with them for nothing. Moreover, that lost time cannot be recovered. So they will blame the other for putting them in this predicament.

Each partner must validate and justify their reason for the break up. So the very first thing they do is go back to the very people who told them the person was worthless and tell them that they were right in their assessement of their partner. That person will say, I told you he or she was no good. They really and truly don't want to hear this preachment but they recognize the fact that it is necessary and must therefore endure the pain in order to shift the blame to the other partner. For the most part most of us don't like to be wrong about anything.

Not once does the person telling the story at any time admits any wrong doing. The person who told them that their partner is or was no good could care less about whether the family member or friend is wrong or right they are more concerned about being right themselves when they originally pronounced the partner was no good.

The spouse telling the story has just set themselves up for a lifetime of continued interference from that family member or friend. For you see given the humans that we are, for the most part, once a person admits that they were wrong about something and the other person was right they will forever be perceived as being dumb. Henceforth, whenever they are involved in a conversation with that person said person will always think that they know what is best for you. Simply put, that person will think that your elevator stops before it reaches the top floor. I guess we all need to be validated in one respect or the other.

How dare you be happy when I am in all of this pain and it is all your fault that I am unhappy. If one or the other hears the other laughing on the phone while talking to a friend there will be hell to pay. How dare you sit around and laugh with others while you treat me like this? Can't you see that I am unhappy and most of all why are you just sitting there and not attempting to correct my problem? You put me in this situation and I hate you for it.

Right then and there a total commitment is made to wreck the other's life by any means necessary. Neither of the two really know the seriousness of their actions they only want to make the other feel just as rejected and dejected as they are. The rejected one must find a way to ensure the other is most unhappy.

At one point in my life I thought that only folks pass the age of twenty-five should be allowed to marry because I thought they would be more mature in handling life's **stresses** and situations. If you look at marriages today there are as many old fools as young ones when it comes to divorces. The expectations are just to difficult to live up to. Its just that simple.

If I understand this marriage commitment thing correctly I am suppose to spend or devote the rest of my life ensuring my partner is happy. What about my personal issues? If I devote my time mainly concerned with my own personal issues and you do likewise, it seems that we would be better off. If after dealing with my own personal monsters and issues if I have any energy left over, I will attempt to assist you with your problems. It must be clearly understood however that I cannot assist you with your issues until I have successfully placed mine in check.

You want me to console you when in fact I am attempting to beat back my own demons. Individuals need to understand one thing in life no one can solve or resolve your personal problems. That strength must come from within yourself. Sure, if I see you struggling with an issue or problem I will make every attempt to let you know that I will be there for you mentally.

In many cases one or the other partner is more mentally needy than the other and will attempt to use the strength of the other to make themselves feel better. This is the worst trap the stronger person can be lured into. If you allow your partner to mentally drain you with all of their needy issues, they will use you up and discord you like a worthless coin. If you detect that your partner is mentally needy encourage them to seek counseling or seek their strength through spiritual healing.

If you knew your perspective spouse was a nut case prior to the marriage why did you marry in the first place? Marriage is much more than sex. Your perspective partner should be at least strong enough to make a few decisions independently without the other's input. The marriage is suppose to be about having someone to share and enjoy life with and not about having someone that you must mentally take care of for the rest of your life.

You and your spouse should be about the raising of your children that is if you have any and not about raising each other. A couple should expect to address the mental and physical needs of their children. How can a household expect to successfully raise a family when one of the spouses require more time and attention than the children. If a person has the notion that they are the center of the universe they should have remained single and not engaged themselves into some false commitments.

What happened to commitment and honesty when you failed to tell me that you were head-over-heels in debt prior to our marriage? You knew I was committed to purchasing a house for our family. What happened to commitment and honesty when you failed to tell me that you had another family to support wherein most of your money goes there?

By all means you should take care of your children from a pervious marriage but you should have been committed and forthright enough to let me know this prior to our marriage. You knew that I expected to live a certain lifestyle, however, with most of your money going to child support I must put my dreams on hold.

Whenever I point these issues out you tell me that I am being unreasonable. No I am not, you out and out used subterfuge in your pursuit of me. Your failure to commitment and honesty has caused undue **stress** on this marriage and it is sitting on a very rocky foundation. Inasmuch as you have placed this unwanted **stress** on me I really can't give you a date and time that this marriage will end.

That's right, end. For how can I trust you to have my back in future situations and look out for me or our family's best interest.

A person's ability to honor a commitment is based on their code of honor. For example, if I am in pursuit of a spouse and I learn that my perspective mate has been married before and if that marriage didn't end in the death of the partner, I would be extremely careful.

If the perspective mate has been married more than once and the marriage didn't end due to the death of the partner, get away from this person as fast as you can by any means necessary. Any person with multi-marriages, commitment code should be carefully examined. Don't be taken in just because the apple has a pretty red color. Looks can be very deceiving and the apple may not be sweet at all. Once you bite the apple and discover worms, better move on.

Even more troubling, if my perspective spouse has been married at least two times and both times the mate died during the course of the marriage, run away fast. Although the situation may have been justified I would not want to go to bed at night thinking that my spouse's pervious mates died during the course of the marriage especially if the person is young. All of my energy should be focused on making my marriage work. In order to have a sound marriage as much **stress** as possible should be eliminated.

In order for me to allow you to understand where I am coming from relative to commitments the below enumerated list should give you an insight of what commitments should be honored.

If you allow me to be myself, I will always be faithful

When we first met I was an individual with a will to conduct my life in a manner that is consistent with my overall make-up. Simply put, I had a freedom to make decisions that were most beneficial to myself. Now should a marriage change that particular aspect of me totally? Well, I don't think so. For if you attempt to change me you will take me out of my natural element thereby creating or placing undue **stress** on me. Resultantly, I just may become something or someone that even I will not be able to recognize.

For example, if you like to live in a very hot house and I like a cool house and you always have the temperature up high. Being the humans that we are, if we can't amicably come to a meeting of the minds sooner or later we will seek comfort elsewhere. Maybe back to your parents' house, but for the most part one wouldn't seek refuge at their parents' house because the parents will tell them just how silly they are being. So where else is there to go, I just wonder?

If you become unable to care for yourself due to physical or mental illness, I commit myself to your well being

This is one commitment that I would have no problem in keeping even if it alters my life and creates additional **stress**. No one has any idea of what the future holds for us. We all need to recognize that any of us at any given time can fall prey to a serious physical or mental disorder. I would have no problem in this regard because the illness or disorder that you encountered could well have befallen me.

Although it appears that in some marriages most folks don't know the real meaning of the word commitment, I think it can best be described by looking at two soldiers during wartime in a foxhole. Both of them recognize the fact that in order for either of them to have any possible chance of survival each of them must somehow do all they can to protect the blind side of the other. In today's society many marriages fail because one partner or the other only want their partner to watch their blind side and to hell with yours'. It is called selfishness.

No matter how much two people love each other selfishness will soon cripple or place undue **stress** on any given marriage. Just like being in the foxhole your partner should recognize the possible dangers that will confront you. I used the war foxhole analogy because marriage is a very serious business.

Even though society has allowed marriages and the failure thereof to become a big joke in this society, said failures can be directly attributed to many of our social ills in this society. What really happens to a child's thinking process when the child sees his parents engaged in the vicious combat associated with a divorce. Sure, we trick ourselves into believing the child will be okay. Are we really serious in that regard? I don't think so.

When parents decide to get a divorce within their hearts and souls they know the children will suffer. To put it bluntly, they don't care for if they did, they would somehow make some type of agreement to ensure they remained together until the child reaches the age of eighteen. Then they could go on their merry ways.

Can't be done you say. Yes it could if the parents weren't so selfish. The most precious element in any society is the children. Just like in the foxhole if I don't protect your back we are going to lose the war. Well in today's society we may just be losing the war because even the government doesn't seem to care about what happens to the children. If it did it would do something about some of the basic root causes that severely affects our children.

Speaking of commitment every jurisdiction in this county should commit itself to making divorces much harder to obtain. Sure in some cases divorces may be necessary. Even then the government must ask itself what are to become of the children of divorced parents. Do we provide the funds up front in an attempt to keep them out of jail or do we wait until the child has done bodily harm to another human being and then provide the funds to keep the child incarcerated.

I commit myself to not making too many commitments

One of the worst things any person can do is to make too many promises especially those that are unreasonable and unable to be fulfilled. If you tell a person something especially something that the person wants to hear they will cling to every word that is said and if you at any time or in any way deviate from your promise it will be held against you. The person may not necessarily directly challenge you about it.

However, you can rest assure that it is being stored in the computer (brain) and at some time, maybe during the course of an argument those very words that you uttered will resurface. At that point you will be called one of the world's worst liars and the person may very well have a good point.

I commit myself to be honest with my partner

For the most part it is the continued little things that breaks up a marriage. Let your partner know about some of the things that annoys you the most. We all have them. Let them know that you love them dearly but you are not comfortable with the way they continues to suck their teeth after eating a meal for example. Let them know however that you understand that they must be themselves and that you are not trying to change them and that you will make every attempt to tolerate it but that it just annoys you.

Convey to them that if during one of those times that you leave the room do not take it personally for I am sure that I must annoy you at some point. Assure them that you are merely attempting to find a comfort level in your daily lives. Assure them that you have no intentions of leaving or abusing them for being themselves. Encourage them to points out some of your habits that annoys them. For we all have a few bad habits that we need to refine.

One must be very careful in this regard. One must realize that no one wants to be perceived as being annoying. One must also remember that some things in life must be tolerated without being mentioned. In order to avoid **stressing** your partner out one can't mention every little thing, somethings will just have to be sucked up. So select your annoyances carefully otherwise the mention of too many can have a deleterious affect on the union.

Till Death Do Us Apart

Are you kidding me? Talk about a cat having nine lives. I have known or heard of people being married more than nine times. I guess with each episode or failed marriage a little bit of the person did in fact die. Therefore, it doesn't take rocket science to conclude that when people talk about "till death do us apart" they surely wasn't talking about an actual physical death. I guess the death of what they were talking about is the death of the love between the two of them.

It has always been amazing to me that two people can at one time look into each other's eyes and stand before a crowd of people and proclaim that they will stay together until the death of one or the other. Even now as I write this I can't help but laugh.

Why is it that whenever a spouse dies for other than natural causes, i.e., mysteriously, violently or any other unknown reason or reasons, the spouse is always the first suspect. Even if the spouse dies of natural causes there will always be a few who will suspect that some sort of misconduct by the other spouse occurred.

Any criminologist will tell you that history has demonstrated that when most marriages goes sour even the most so-called respected in our society have shown a propensity to rid themselves of the albatross that they perceive to be holding them back. Usually the spouse.

The culprit in this regard will clearly know that by carrying out the evil deed of ridding themselves of their evil spouse, death would have surely parted them. In most cases of this nature the culprit is in such haste to rid themselves of the other that there is no need for a Sherlock holmes or Dr. Lee. The evidence leading up to the crime will be so apparent that an elementary student can solve the crime.

I am talking about intelligent people, lawyers, doctors, judges, police officers, etc. The **stress** of the bad marriage is so great that they lose sight of all reasonal objectives thereby making it so easy to be caught. Of course they vehemently deny their action and some even convince themselves that what they did was justified. Therefore, to them they tell themselves that they are innocent.

The need to relieve themselves of the **stress** was so compelling that they would ruin their entire lives. Go to any prison in this country and you will be amazed at the number of people incarcerated due to violence in one form or the other occurring in the home. What happened to the love and where did it go? The love disappeared because you wanted me to be a clone of you and when I failed to completely acquiesce in that regard you started to hate me.

Inasmuch as I failed to become you, you felt that you would expedite the process of death doing us part. Instead of the love we felt at the beginning of our relationship we started to feel hate and disgust toward one another. If only we had been mature enough to realize that I cannot be you and you cannot be me we may have had a chance to survive or at least be able to tolerate each other.

Even by changing partners if one doesn't understand the basic principle that no one can live for another or make another completely happy they will encounter the same problems in future relationships.

The most basic question that one can ask relative to the abuse by a spouse is what would cause a seemingly reasonable and rational person to actually invent a plan to take the life of their partner. Greed or money could be a motive. Believe it or not the motive may not center around either of those reasons.

The two most powerful emotions known to man is **LOVE** and **HATE.** We have all heard of the saying that love will make one do foolish things. We must always remember that for every action there is an equal and opposite reaction. Inasmuch as love can make one do foolish things the same can be said of hate with the same intensity. For the most part when most of us feel that our personal space has been violated we must take some action to correct the situation.

No matter how you slice it, it gets back to not allowing a person to be themselves. If you can't do the things that I want you to do you must be eliminated. If you cannot become me and adhere to my way of thinking you therefore serve no useful purpose in my life and you must be eliminated. Instead of just walking away you must be punished for your failure to think as I do. Sadly, in a lot of cases it just doesn't stop there.

The culprit must visit some of the spouse's relatives to make them suffer too for knowing you. When it is all over and the motive is examined. Sometimes the motive is so stupid that all one can do is shake their head in disgust. Had the love remained as strong as the hate became it would have been a great union.

In the not so distant past every law enforcement jurisdiction in this country had to rewrite their domestic abuse laws. There was a time in this country that a spouse could literally beat or maim their spouse and little or nothing would be done. Even if the partner was wounded so badly that hospitalization was required the prosecutor sometimes would not seek an indictment.

There was a time in this country that if the police was called to a home to investigate a report of domestic violence even if the officers saw blood on one of the subjects, bruises or other obvious signs of inappropriate conduct nothing would be done. The officers would separate the two and tell them to stop it. For the most part the only time an arrest would be made was if one actually killed the other.

During those years if a spouse beat or maim their partner within an inch or two of their life and the culprit was arrested and subsequently went to court, which would sometimes take more than a month or two, all charges would more than likely be dropped or dismissed. During the interim the two would have completely made up and resolved their differences for the moment relative to that particular incident. The prosecutor would thereby dismiss the charges due to the lack of a witness.

I am truly glad to say that those times in this country have since passed. Domestic violence is now taken very seriously in this country. Matter of fact a great number of jobs will not hire an individual if he or she has been convicted of domestic violence. No law enforcement entity will hire anyone who has a domestic violence conviction nor will the army take anyone in that regard. In many cases a company may even fire or dismiss an individual if it becomes known that said individual has a domestic violence conviction.

Still with all the strict laws against domestic violence in place everyday somewhere in this country a police office is dispatched to a home for a report of domestic violence. The question must therefore be asked is it a natural tendency for mankind to be violent.

As I said earlier this violence things affects people from every walk of life. Look around you at no time in your lifetime was there peace throughout the world. Throughout our life time there has and continues to be some conflict in some part of the world where lives are being taken due to violence. Look at our country violent crimes are always present.

Now I am not a psychologist but I will venture to say that if mankind is serious about addressing our violent behavior it must start with the children. I don't even know given man's history if violence can be eradicated. Maybe that is just the way man was made. Getting back to the children. It all starts with the family. When you have two so-called mature married adults who cannot resolve the most simplist disagreement without violence coming into play, what message does this send to our children who's minds are no where near the adult's developmental stage?

So tell yourself the children will be okay resultant to a divorce the only thing the parents have done is plant the seed for violence. One of the things that their divorce conduct has demonstrated is the fact that if you can't resolve a problem, run and if someone stand in your way run over them. If they happen to get hurt while you are attempting to run well, they should not have been in your way. The child easily learn that in order for him/her to survive he/she must take each and every necessary precaution to protect themselves.

Where is the love and where did it go? Children should be taught that sure mankind will have differences but in order to live in this world peaceably we must put aside our selfishness and come to the realization that more people besides themselves live on this planet and we must all attempt to get along. One good step in that direction is not to make getting a divorce such as easy endeavor.

Throughout history mankind has demonstrated a propensity to extract revenge for anything that he perceives to cause harm to him in any manner by others. Be it disrespect, disloyalty, failure to acknowledge he is God, failure to agree with him, etc. In most cases man not only wants revenge he must have some blood.

For example, even the government will seek revenge by killing another human being. At least one thing should ring abundantly clear killing is killing no matter the source. If the government can so-call legally kill another human being how can the same government condemn another for killing. In each scenario you are talking about a body of men or a man making a decision to kill another. It is not like God came from heaven and decided to kill the culprit. Inasmuch as man cannot make life how can it ever be justified that any man can knowingly take another's life.

It is apparent to me that everyone is not on the same mental level, as such we will all walk away with our own opinions on any subject matter. We say that violence on the television is wrong and children shouldn't watch it. Yet, on that same television the government will sentence another human being to die. What is more violent than that? Conduct of that nature does not deter crime it only plants a seed in someone's mind that if others can kill so can I. Especially in the minds of impressionable little children. It is a never ending tune that keeps repeating itself.

Love Addiction

Everyone in this country with any amount of reasonable intelligence is familiar with the term drug addict. In the context that the phrase is used I will venture to say that my own personal definition of the word addict simply means someone who loves any particular matter be it real or imagined, more than they love themselves and will do anything to gain possession or control of said matter at any and all cost even death.

I can take you or you can go into any city in this country and you will find a drug addict. On the same hand, you can go into any city in this country and find a love addict lurking around somewhere. Both of these two are extremely dangerous. Never thought of that from that perspective have you. The statistics will prove my point. On any given night in any city you will have as many or more arrest for domestic violence as drug arrest.

Remember my definition addiction is all about control, in the context of domestic violence, it is all about control. If I can't control you I will use my physical might to make you acquiesce with my desires. If my physical prowess do not equal yours I will use whatever weapon or object I can find to stack the odds in my favor.

Just like the drug addict during the course of domestic violence the parties lose all sense of self and something within themselves tells them that they must win in this situation or all will be lost. At that moment they will do anything to prevail.

If you observe a junkie in the pursuit of his/her drugs you will see the very same face on the domestic abuser, the very same intense desire to get control of the situation that will make them whole. They could care less about the cost during that moment and if you in any way attempt to impede them, they just may kill you. Sure, after the fact they will tell everyone how sorry they are and promise to never allow themselves to commit the same act again. That is until the next time when the very cycle is repeated.

Having said that I just keep wondering as I may have said earlier, is man just prone to violence and each and everyone of us is just waiting for the right episode or situation to manifest itself so we can go into our animalistic act. If violence is inherent in man we can't say that we are acting as animals when so-called uncharacteristic behavior surfaces. If man is prone to violence we would therefore be acting like humans and by saying we sometimes act like animals we really don't want to face our true reality. Scary.

Speaking of animals throughout my teen and adult life I have always been fascinated by animal life and behavior. I can sit and watch the lions and hyenas all day. What I am about to talk about really saddens me. In watching some of those shows I sometimes see man acting in the same exact way.

From what I have gleaned in watching the lions each pride is controlled by a big ferocious male lion who will protect all the females and ensure all of their physical needs and desires are met. From time to time other male lions will challenge the male leader for the ownership of his pride. If the incumbent loses he is either killed or driven from the pride in shame.

When the new leader takes control one of the first things he does is kill and eat all of the young clubs that were fathered by the former leader while the females of the pride stand idly by. Natures way I guess and that is the way it is supposed to be. What I am getting at is this. In our present day society you have some women who's former lover have left them for whatever reasons who will take up with another lover and allow that lover to abuse the children that were fathered by another man. Unlike the lion they sometimes will not stand idly by but assist in the abuse just to gain points and favor with the new lover.

Women like this due to their love addiction will do anything to be on good terms with their man. I can't think of a more horrendous act. It really saddens me to know that a human being could love someone more than they love their children. If someone wants to make a fool of themselves that is all well and good but why make the children suffer. That statement was not intended to single out women for a deadbeat dad is equally as bad in my opinion.

Cases of this nature happens too often for them to be isolated incidents. In talking about matters of this nature one might ask why should I dwell on such morbid issues. One must understand that in this life especially if we want to address issues relevant to everyday life every aspect of life must be examined. Failure to examine all aspects will only serve to increase the problems related to the situation.

While growing up and during the time I was learning about the birds and the bees as we like to say I could never understand why some females were attracted to the bad guys. Then on the other hand some males were attracted to the bad girls. You know, the guys who had absolutely no respect for female hood seemed to be the most popular.

Just like the drug addict the love addict will love someone else more than they love themselves and their children. More often than not the love addict just like the drug addict clearly knows that their lifestyle is detrimental to their safety, yet they continue in that way of life. The drug addict knows that the drugs are no good for him/her, yet their ever waking moments are all about the pursuit of drugs.

The love addict clearly knows that the person they are pursuing is no good for them, yet they do not possess the strength to tear themselves from the chains that binds them. It doesn't matter what family, friends and relatives may say nothing will stop the behavior until said person come to the realization of the destructive behavior and attempts to change it. Then in some cases the damage is so extensive that it will take years and years to recover. In some cases they never recover.

If the addict is addicted to an extremely or over selfish person just like the drug addict they will be in for the worst ride of their lives. The person that they are addicted too will show no mercy or compassion in the way they will treat the other. Matter of fact to them it is just one big joke to know that they have another human being who will do everything that is commanded of them. They will engage in other relationships and the addict knows about them, yet the addict does not have the will-power to do anything about it. In most cases the addict can expect be beaten or abused in some form of the other on a daily basis.

Even if the beatings happen to leave obvious signs of abuse to the extent that others may notice it they will lie and say that they fell down the stairs or walked into a door. Others will tell them of the dangers that confronts them and yet they will say that they will be alright. Even if the abuser is confronted by friends and relatives the abuser will say that he or she is doing nothing wrong and the other person is free to leave at anytime they want to. The abuser knows that the abusee will not leave because they are clearly addicted.

Then one day from out of the blue a little light may go off in the abused brain and they may resort to serious violence. The next thing you know the abuser is dead. Just like the abusee didn't like themselves the opposite occurred and with the same degree of hatred for self, that hatred was turned toward the abuser. Imagine the abuser attempting to plead his case for mercy when they clearly knows by the look on the abused face that their time is about up.

It probably would go something like this, that is if the abuser is given the opportunity to even address the issue. In many cases the abuser is killed or maimed while they are drunk or asleep. As the abuser stands there looking down the barrel of a small hand gun which by the way, appears to be a cannon, their mind hastely attempt to find words to abort this situation. The abuser knows certain key words to say that might bring the abused back under control. After a few phrases are uttered and nothing happens the abuser knows that this is a very serious situation.

The abuser attempts to talk about some of the good moments which were very few for the abusee, yet nothing happens, the gun is pointed in the abuser's direction. The abuser will tell the abusee how different things are going to be in the future and all the wonderful changes that will be forthcoming. Again no reaction. The abuser sees the grip tighten on the gun handle and sweat begins to pour as if the abuser is in a shower.

The abuser will tell the abusee that he/she has already started to change and request that the abused look into his/her jacket pocket and the abused will find two tickets for a show and dinner. The abuser is making an attempt to create a distraction so the gun can be removed from the abused hand. Still no reaction. It must be noted at this point that in some cases the abuser is able to talk themselves out of the situation. Usually when that happens the abuser will use the same gun on the abusee. The abuser reason that this person had the nerve to make an attempt on their life.

The abuser will promise to do everything that is asked of him/her for as long as they live. Still no reaction. The abuser sees the finger tightening on the trigger. The abuser then falls to their knees and invoke the name of God and begs for mercy. Where was all the mercy when the abuser was doing all the evil deeds toward the abused? Where was all the mercy when the abuser treated the abused as if they didn't have any feelings?

Just before the flash from the barrel the abuser thinks back on what could have been had time been given to cultivate a sound and reasonable relationship. Many people would have given their right arm to be involved with someone who's every waking moment was the thought and obligation to make them happy. Had the abuser at any time in the relationship just taken a little time to say thank you or just demonstrate a small amount of appreciation, said abuser could have remained king or queen for the rest of their life.

However, just like in most cases most of us don't really know what we have until we are about to lose it. All to often as humans we never really appreciate all the good and simple things in life until they are gone. Then on the other hand some of us are like that and some of us do not possess the ability to recognize and appreciate a good thing. Inasmuch as it takes all kinds to make the world it therefore stands to reason that some among us will be abusers and on the other end of the spectrum some will be the abused. Like in the case of the lions can humans really do anything about our situation?

Just before the flash the abuser launches toward the gun and that is the abuser's final act. The abusee at that time felt no pain nor regret because the abusee was already dead. They had no life and everything within them had long since died. Even while in court their reality of things was so clouded that they were unable to discern right from wrong. They only knew that a big burden had been removed from their life and they no longer felt that addiction.

Even if the abuser had been the one to have pulled the trigger the abuser would not have been able to discern right from wrong because all of the reasoning ability would have been focused on the fact that the abusee had the nerve to defy a given commands.

The Games They Play

Beginning with the early years of school students are taught about the various games people played and viewed as a form of sports or for entertainment. The most notable in this regard were always centered around the Romans. Even today we must still be entertained in one form or the other, i.e., football, basketball, etc. If the entertainment is not competitive enough to the extent that some blood is spilled from time to time we become bored.

In our everyday lives we are competitive with each other. If you drive to work you can't let that car get in front of you. My house must be as big or bigger than yours'. I must make more money than you do. I must always be number one. It is all about I, I, I, or me, me.

When a marriage is started, initially the couple may have the intent of sharing things and becoming this so-call oneness thing but as time passes they will resort back to their true selves. Selfishness. One can only play that oneness game for so long. Each one in their own right will begin to chart a course to gain control over the other. If the **stress** of this attempted change is too great on either party serious problems will occur.

Given man's propensity to selfishness why should he listen to anyone when in fact he thinks that he knows everything. If the couple can't come to or learn how to compromise the marriage is doomed. Marriages that last are the ones wherein the couples learn to agree to disagree with the one stipulation that adultery is totally forbidden. There goes that oneness thing. I can't be you nor can you be me. The sooner we both come to that realization the better off we will both be. Matter of fact why should one want to be like someone else anyway?

I was attracted to you because I saw something in you that was totally different from myself. Had I wanted a clone of myself, I should have remained by myself. I recognize the fact that I don't want to just live and die as a lonely old person. I recognize that as I get older I will need someone to spend those golden years with. You can rest assured that it will not be the young folks spending that much time with older folks because they will have their own lives and that is the way it should be.

It therefore stands to reason that we should stop all of these mind games and be about the business of just trying to live. What I just said is totally worthless to a young couple in their teens and twenties. One, they have no concept about being or getting old they think that they will remain young forever and can therefore change partners whenever the going gets a litte tough.

Getting back to my games scenario. When some couples get married they seem to think that they can train or teach their spouse as if they would a little child. For example, if while growing up I became accustomed to placing or putting my shoes in a certain place and you on the other hand is accustomed to having shoes in a certain place look for a problem. Before I go any further, you might ask why am I talking about something that has such little meaning? Wrong, everything in a marriage has a meaning.

Simply put, when you get married and start living together your every waking moment impacts your partner's life. When I say or talk about everything I mean just that. Things like shoes although which may seem to be a small issue can certainly escalated into a much larger one. It isn't really the shoes it is the **stress** of having to deal with the shoe issue on a daily basis.

I am certain that you have heard of people getting into trouble with the law for what appeared to be stupid issues. For example, people have been harmed for as little as someone taking a penny from them. Now we all know the value of a penny. The trouble did not arise due to the value of the penny but rather, the issues surrounding the penny.

Within the human species the competitiveness and selfishness is so profound that we deduce that if someone or anyone does anything to challenge or take advantage of us a certain amount of revenge must be doled out. In a marriage whenever one party is hurt or feels that they were in some way disrespected, being the humans that we are, we will invent a plan or scheme to extract revenge no matter how subtle and that can be a major problem.

In life there are certain degrees of endurance that affects each and every one of us differently. When I hatch my so-called revenge scheme based on what I believe to be a subtle approach I have no way to factor how my plan for revenge may affect my partner. Usually when a person is attempting to get even with a spouse for being mistreated in some way or the other the punishment more often than not, is not intended to do long term harm unless of course they actually intend to do physical harm.

This game is played back and forth and each time punishment is doled out the intensity of the situation mounts until it is out of hand. At that point hate actually begin to take root. When things reaches that point someone is subject to be seriously hurt either physically or mentally. In some cases the competitive jucies are so intense that one or the other will use the children in an attempt to gain an advantage.

One or the other may tell the children that the other treats them badly and children being who they are just might begin to actually develop a hatred toward the other parent. It doesn't stop there some will even inflict self made wounds in an attempt to validate their point. When matters reach this point and the family is so dysfunctional, anything is subject to occur from some form of injury or even death. As these games are being played no one actually takes the time to evaluate the situation to prevent the on-set of potential violence.

Both parties are just so intent on getting their way in matters that an outsider would consider to be frivolous issues. After the fact when someone is hurt or injured they wish that they had put their pride aside and just walked away. Sorry, too late. You can't un-ring the bell nor can one change what has happened in the past. It is therefore essential that we all from time to time take the time to find tune our minds on what is actually important in our daily lives and adhere to them accordingly.

I will admit that I play mind games with myself but my games centers around safety issues. For example, when I am out and about in the general public I make an attempt to tell myself that the most important thing or issue that I must address is my safe return to home base. Given the violence and the ever increasing amount of **stress** in our society it doesn't take much to find one self in a position where one is being challenged about something. Again, more often than not it will be something that in hindsight will be considered stupid. A person may cut you off in traffic or the cashier didn't give you the correct amount of change.

Whenever I am confronted with one of those situations I tell myself to remain peaceful because it is more important to get back home rather than to engage in this conversation. Sometimes it works and sometimes it doesn't. Sometimes matter escalates so rapidly that before we know it we are heavily engaged in a verbal altercation. One in which if one or the other doesn't return to a common sense mode something bad will happen and both parties will surely regret it.

Sometimes while in public it appears that some folks are out there to engage in a confrontaion with other people. Maybe their significant other did something to piss them off and they must find a way to vent their frustration. Maybe their boss pissed them off. Whatever the reason it is a dangerous game. The person they may encounter just may be suffering from the same affliction and in cases of this nature more often than not, violence may occur.

Not too many people in our society want to be viewed as being a coward. As such, some of us will do everything in our power to avoid that stigma. The question then begs is it better to be a live coward or a dead hero? What good is a dead hero to his or her family? What good is a dead hero to his children and the rest of his or her family? Don't get me wrong there are times that one must take a stand. I served in the military and would have given my life for my country. I am talking about frivolous matters.

When I talk about going home to avoid a confrontation. I am talking about going to a place where one can feel that they are the king or queen of the castle. Even in a marriage each partner should select an area within their house that they can call their personal space or home. I will talk about that later. Just like in the public when one is angry with the spouse they need to retreat to their safety zone to avoid a confrontation. For you see the spouse just may be in a bad mood and need someone to kick around or pick on and at that moment you, the cat, the dog or anyone else will do.

If you happen to be in the general area you will receive the full raft of their frustration. Which is a very dangerous game because the other partner just may be experiencing the same frustration at the very same time. The boss or the children may have pissed them off too. As they stand there venting, issues that were not addressed some six to eight months ago just may surface. They started out by arguing about the milk not being put back in the refrigerator and now everything is open for discussion. Well I shouldn't call it a discussion because usually no meaningful resolution can be reached during these times.

In so many cases the marriage is doomed before it has a chance to develop into a meaningful union. We sometimes have a tendency to present ourselves as something we are not while in the pursuit of that someone special. Trouble begins to loom around every corner when the significant other really find out that the person was just playing a game to win their affection.

In my marriage I have always been wary whenever my spouse attempts call me pet names that she doesn't usually call me. My argument in this regard is really simple. When my spouse is angry at me for whatever reason I am then a SOB or some other foul name. Just maintain the consistency. If you want something of me or want to induce me to do a certain thing just say or ask it and I am more apt to do it.

I really believe that not too many reasonably intelligent people like to be patronized. Not too many people that I know personally like to feel that they were manipulated into doing a certain thing or task. Just keep it all real. That particular tactic maybe acceptable in getting a child to adhere to authority but with adults it only serves to make the person resentful of you. When that happens you have created a situation wherein the person will wonder how many other times they have been manipulated. The trust will slowly erode.

The Thrill Of The Chase

If you don't possess the furious bark and can't run with the big dogs you will be better served by remaining in the yard or staying on the porch. A dog will chase a moving vehicle from sun up to sun down and when the vehicle comes to a halt, the dog doesn't know what to do with it. The dog had no plan in mind just knew that it was a moving object and it had to be pursued. Even if the vehicle moves again the dog will chase with the same vigor and intensity. That cycle will repeat itself for as long as the vehicle and the dog are in the same area.

Why would the dog expend so much energy in an attempt to caught the vehicle knowing full well that no plans were formulated to deal with the aftermath? The answer is really simple it was just the thrill of the chase. Even if the vehicle was filled with a deadly material the dog would continue the chase with the same amount of vigor. It matters not that the vehicle maybe detrimental to the health and well being of the dog the chase must go on no matter the cost.

With some humans it seems to be no different. Just like the dog some humans will chase anything of the opposite sex that moves. Well in this day and age it is okay to say even of the same sex if the individual is so inclined. No time or thought is given to the substance or character of the individual just got to have them. Some while in pursuit of that special someone will place too much emphasis on all the wrong things.

More often than not it will be how the person looks rather than what type of human being the person is. As a small kid growing up with my peers we often said that we would never ever marry a beautiful woman because the competition to maintain and keep her would be too fierce. Now this is not intended to put down beautiful women because any human being be they so-called ugly or beautiful with their head on straight can be an asset to their partner.

Whenever two individuals are attracted to each other they should be honest with each other regarding their likes and dislikes. For as sure as you are reading this a person's true self will surface and for the most part your partner will turn against you for misrepresenting yourself. That works both ways.

If you start out with the flowers or chocolate thing don't think that you can stop once you are married. Matter of fact the less you do will serve you better in the long run. So what if you don't win the person it is better to lose early in the game rather than after you have invented all of your money, time and effort.

If the stupid dog had any sense he or she would just wait and approach the vehicle after it has stopped. That way it would have been able to reserve some of that energy to investigate the worth of the vehicle. Some of us are the same way after we have expended so much energy on the chase we really have nothing substantive to offer. As such, we must make up lies to win the person.

The person being pursued becomes so engrossed in the attention of the chase that they too become accustomed to the attention and the many lies that are being told. In an attempt to keep the chase interesting the pursuee will sometimes increase the pace. At this point they are both in never-never land and when they attempt to come back to reality neither of them can figure out the true essence of their actual being. Subsequently, they begin to hate each other for leading them down this what they thought to be a primrose lane.

The actual truth of the matter is they are both to embarrassed to face each other for being such fools. If they had acknowledged to each other that they were attracted to each other they could have spent all of that wasted time attempting to find a way to coexist with each other in a peaceful way. Had they been able to just keep it real they wouldn't have to endure the pain of being such fools. I am more than certain that you have heard the phrase all that gliters may not necessarily be gold. Even if it is gold one has to pursue it with honesty. For if it is ever discovered that your chase was based on fraudulent reasons you will forever have a credibility problem and the person you are pursuing may never fully trust you again.

Each time you attempt to make a suggestion your partner will wonder if you have some other motive in mind. Over a period of time this continued mindset will bring about undue **stress** and all of your actions will be scrutinized. Now if you are a person who likes to be chased go ahead and enjoy every second of it. However, just remember that one day sooner or later the chase must end. It may be due to age of some other reason.

Separate But Equal

As a kid growing up I always liked candy. However, my family didn't have the financial ability to keep me and my sibling supplied in that regard. I always wished that I could work in a candy store that way I figured that I would be able to comsume all the candy that I wanted whenever I wanted it. Be careful of what you wish for. Well I did get the opportunity to work in a place that sold candy and for first week or so my entire small childhood salary which wasn't very much was used to pay off my candy debt.

Well after eating so much candy there came a time in my life that I started to hate candy. Over exposure you might say. At that young age I couldn't understand for the life of me how I could love candy so much one day and with the passage of a twenty-four hour period hate and despise it. When I had acquired the ability to have as much as I wanted, after a period of time I had no need or desire for it. Even being near it had no appreciable affect on me.

In hindsight I must attribute those desires as being part of the overall chases in life. Like the dog it was my wish to have the candy at my disposal without a plan to treat it with care and most importantly, to treat it in such a way as to avoid a hatred for it. Had I not desired the candy so much at the time, I probably would have continued to like it.

In life we all have certain things that we desire and the only way to get or keep those desires from consuming us is to be very careful and not let our desires overrule our common sense. That's just the way life is. Even when we are pursuing or chasing a partner we have certain desires that we envision as being in that person. When our mind's eye sees or detect that in an individual we will chase that person to the very end of the earth if necessary. Even sometimes if the person shows no interest in our advances we will sometimes continue the chase. That is where one's actions and pursuit can become a violation of the law. Stalking.

Even the person that is being pursued have their own personal desires that are as germane to them as yours are to you. As such, it is therefore safe to conclude that all of us have certain desires that must be fulfilled. Otherwise life has no meaningful purpose. Most of our desires, wants and needs are embedded or ingrained within us over a period of years. Thusly, it is therefore safe to conclude that it is almost impossible for a person to meet and marry another without taking their past history with them.

All the wedding vows or promises that one may make during an actual marriage ceremony will not change the fact that one must first be themselves. Likewise, your partner must be themselves. The most important task that challenges the marriage will be the ability, knowledge and understanding on how to make it work. In other words when two people enters or agree to be married they are both separate and given that fact, their goal should be how to live together on equal terms.

In order for both parties to survive a certain amount of, I should say that a great amount of individuality must be maintained. If not the marriage is doomed to fail. Their primary goal should be to establish certain rules that they both plan to adhere too in order to strengthen the family base. The situation will be much better when it is established and understood that the two of them are different and will not and connot do things in the same manner. However, one thing is clear. The rent or mortage must be paid on a monthly basis. The same is true for all of the other bills.

Once that understanding is made clear and the two have established parameters to reach their desired objectives it shouldn't really matter what or how each of them view how they go about completing their objectives.

If a rich kid is born who likes candy as much as the poor kid and the rich kid can buy or have as much candy as he or she wants and if the rich kid overinduldge in the eating of the candy just like the poor kid, sooner or later the rich kid will develop the same harted as the poor kid did. Too much access or overinduldgence will turn almost any of us against a certain thing.

With the poor kid, life presented a challenge in his or her quest to obtain the candy. With the rich kid it was never a challenge and therefore the rich kid just took it for granted that he or she was just entitled to it. Ever wonder why poor folks don't commit suicide as often as rich folks. Well after the rich folks have accomplished everything in life it is sometimes no longer a challenge for them and they have nothing to look forward to.

On the other hand, poor folks have nothing and everyday presents a challenge to obtain something. At this point you may say that I have gotten away from my point and I am now rambling. The point that I am attempting to make is the fact that no matter who we are we all have separate but equal issues.

Separate Bedrooms

My talking about the candy issue was a deliberate attempt by me to get you to understand the significance of what I am about to talk about now. It is often said that in order to keep your mate it would behoove one to do the very same things that it took to win their affections at the beginning of the relationship. Well I agree with that in part.

Lets just go back to the beginning of a relationship any relationship. At some point two people looked at each other and decided that they wanted to spend the rest of their lives together. At that point in the relationship the squeezing of the tooth paste was not an issue. To simplify my point I will just list a few things that were not issues when the two met and if any of the listed issues are not treated with sensitivity they can destroy any marriage. Albeit they may seem to be stupid matters or issues the continued **stress** of dealing with them will doom the marriage.

I already mentioned the tooth paste issue

Putting the toilet paper on the roller in the bathroom

For some people the tissue **must** be placed on the roll in a downward spiral. For others they may prefer the upward spiral. Me, I am a downward spiral person and that doesn't make me wrong or right. I am just thankful that my spouse just happened to also be a downward spiral person. I reason that inasmuch as the gravitational pull of earth is downward it is much easier to pull something downward than upward. During those times that I need toilet paper I want that task accomplished with as little ease as possible. Yes, I am somewhat fanatical when it come to my toilet paper. Why am I talking about things of this nature you might ask? Simple, whenever you attempt to live with someone else everything becomes an issue and must be appropriately addressed.

Your loud snoring
Your failure to listen to me
You put your friends' interest ahead of mine
Your failure to lower the toilet seat after usage
Your constant nagging about the toilet seat
Your refusal to turn off the lights after usage
Your constant nagging about the lights
Your refusal to place your shoes where they belong
Your failure to turn the television off
You disrupt my sleep when you get up during the night
You smother me with all of your unwanted attention

You ignore me

This is a very serious one. As a child I was told the story of Adam and Eve in the garden. From what I gleaned from that story although Eve was clearly warned to stay from a certain tree and inasmuch as Adam was always away taking care of his prescribed business Eve felt as though she was being ignored. During those times it wasn't like she could volunteer with the local redcross or join some women's group. One day while feeling bored and ignored she ventured into the forbidden zone and started talking to you know who. You know the rest of the story. That statement was not intended to put down women for a man probably would have done the very same thing had he been in Eve's position.

If your spouse ever tells you that they are feeling that they are being ignored and feels lonely within the relationship and you have knowingly done everything in your power to satisfy their needs in that regard your spouse will eventually venture into that forbidden zone. You may as well just keep your bags packed for you will be needing them much sooner than you think. The list could goes on and on but I will stop there. I think you get the picture.

If it is true that one must do the same things to keep a mate as they did to get them a serious question must be asked. Where was the person sleeping when you met them? Where ever they were sleeping it was not in your bedroom. On your first few dates during the chase period it was difficult for you to keep that person out of your mind. Your every thought centered around that person.

Your every and only thoughts were centered around you being able to win their affections so you could eventually take them to your bed. I hope you are beginning to see the comparison with the candy issue. At that time you were not concerned with any of the aforementioned issues. When you finally won and took them home the chase was over and after a while your interest started to shift elsewhere. It had to because the chase was now over.

Your partner senses that you are no longer as attentive as you were before. In others words, in their words, you have changed. The fact of the matter is no one has really changed they are now being themselves. As I said earlier every human being on this planet needs a certain amount of space and time to deal with their own personal inner monsters. Just because I entered into your bedroom doesn't make me become you.

When you met me I was living in my own bedroom and after each date it was difficult for us to part from each other. In an attempt to keep those flames burning why can't we continue to keep our separte bedrooms in our one house. For you see in order for us to maintain an interest in each other we must continue to keep the desire for each other alive. When I moved into your bedroom you only took me for granted. Sure, if we have our separate bedroom you can visit me whenever you want to, but sometime during the night you must return to your room. I may allow you to sleep over a few nights but don't get use to that.

Sounds crazy you say that married people don't do things like that. Maybe the fact that they don't have separate bedroom is one of the causes for so many divorces. By agreeing to have our own bedrooms we will eliminate some of the **stress** associated with many of the aforementioned issues. Moreover, we will keep this dating mentality alive.

When we were dating you couldn't get enough of me. We have already committed ourselves to remain faithful to each other so that should not be an issue. We must now find a way to remain married for the duration and raise our children and ensure that they have both parents by their side as it should be. Knowing the way that we love each other we should explore any and all reasonable ways to keep our marriage alive.

Not only should we have separate bedrooms, we should also have separate bathrooms. I can't think of a more private moment in life. I want dwell on it but you know exactly what I am talking about. If your household can afford it always try to have at least three bathrooms. Two if it's only you and your spouse. You need a bathroom for yourself, your spouse and one for the children. If financially possible you need one for the boys and one for the girls.

That way you can maintain automony over every aspect of your assigned area including putting the toilet paper on the roller as you deem appropriate. No I am not saying that you can't use my bedroom or bathroom. I am merely saying that when you enter you have no right to complain about the manner in which I keep it. It must be understood that each of us are individuals and in order to feel worthwhile we must maintain control over something.

Lets not stop there. When you met me I had complete control over my checking account. When we entered into this marriage we knew that certain obligations had to be satisfied. Please know that I will give or spend every cent of my hard earned money on you and my family. However, inasmuch as I work to earn my money I must feel that I have a certain amout of say on how it is to be spent.

So lets do this, we will both maintain banking accounts with each of us being the primary owner on our respective accounts. Of course both of our names will be on the accounts in the event some sort of emergency arises. However, we agree to maintain control of our respective account. No, this is not an attempt to hide or conceal funds from you but rather an attempt to allow you to feel that you are in control. If this marriage is to survive we must trust each other enough to do the right thing. That is very important.

Even if you are a housewife or househusband that doesn't work each of us will still maintain our separate accounts. If the other partner does not work outside the home a certain amount of funds will be set aside for them to have complete control over. In every relationship it is essential that each individual feel that they are part of the overall union. One can't be led around as a child and the other partner expects them to be happy.

Before your partner met you, you had a life and if you married him/her you must have thought that he/she possessed a reasonable amount of intelligence. Or was it just lust. For if it was just lust you may as well keep your bags packed too.

When agreeing to have separate bedrooms also agree that during those times of heated arguments that one partner can retreat to the safety of their respective bedroom and the other partner will respect the other's privacy. This is very important. If you notice I didn't say if a heated argument occurs. For just as sure as you are reading this you will have a few heated arguments. The secret to maintaining the marriage and keeping it intact is knowing where to draw the line.

If during the course of an argument one party decides that enough has been said and retreats to their room, please respect that. For just as sure as the conversation continues, domestic violence can easily occur and that goes for any household. I served in the military during the Vietnam war and I remember that during that time officials had established zones where no fighting would occur known as the DMZ. How stupid, if they could agree not to fight in certain zones it seems that they could have agreed not to fight at all. Then on the other hand that is not the nature of man he must have a fight or two going on somewhere, even in the home.

If after agreeing not to cross a no fight zone in your home and one partner or the other crosses that line you may as well pack your bag and keep it packed, for not too long, your partner will be physically violating you. Most physical confrontations can be avoided if during the course of an argument one partner or the other just stop and think for a moment. Let me give you some very good advice relative to arguments. If during the course of an argument one partner decides to leave the house to gain control of their emotions that partner is either cheating or will start to cheat in the very near future.

I will tell you why I say that. First of all, when we are angry we may do many things that we wouldn't normally do and may regret them later after the fact. When a person is angry they want revenge and they are also vulnerable and susceptible to be preyed upon by other unscrupulous characters. If you want the marriage to last attempt to work out your problems in the home or seek professional counseling.

Believe it or not some of the folks that you may be attempt to confide in may be the very same person that is and has been jealous of you and in the back of their mind want to take or ruin everything that you have. That same person may be the very same person who has been secretly desiring your husband or wife for a number of years. All of a sudden the opportunity is presented to them to destroy your relationship.

They will go along with all the bad things that you may say about your significant other and if you run out of bad things to say, they will insinuate themselves into the picture by yeasting up all the bad things that can be said. All the while they are hoping that you will sooner rather than later leave your partner so they can make their own personal pitch for him/her.

You would really be surprised at the number of people who you think likes you that actually hate your guts. That is why family is so important. Even some family members may hate you. In life we must be very careful and select our partners with extreme care.

One of the most important lessons that can be learned from life is the fact that nature created all of us with our own uniqueness. If nature intended for us to become one with each other we would have been made as such. So if it takes having separate bedrooms to be in touch with ourselves so be it. Just understand that when we marry it should be our objective to raise our children and try to the best of our ability to try to comfort each other during our times of dispair.

One or the other partner should never use the other's weakness to gain any advantage points. For just like one is riding high today or really feeling good about themselves, at any moment nature can create a situation where everything will just seem to fall apart.

In life as well as in a marriage one must be given the necessary room to keep in touch with their own personal monster and demons. Some among us handles that task better than others. If we fail to recognize that we need personal time then all may be lost. When I say personal time I do not mean hanging out all times of night with the boys or girls. When one is married you work out or deal with your dispair in the home or at a counselor's office.

Oh, I almost forgot to mention something of vital importance. The television, especially during the football season. I don't know what it is about the television that will cause every man that I spoke with including myself to channel surf. We cannot not just tune into a station and let it remain there. We must switch from channel to channel in hopes of finding what I don't really know. This just infuriates the wife.

So if you want any peace watching television it would behoove you to have at least three in the house. This way you can watch two games at the same time while your spouse watches what she wants to. Even then she will become angry because you have access to three. You know what happens next.

The main challenge confronting any marriage should not be whether two people can merge together and become one but rather can two people live together and become one plus one. Which in my book becomes two. If three people are in the equation then it will become three, etc., etc.

Marketability Factor

There was a time in my life when I was much younger and if I happened attend a beauty contest and if I saw an eighty year old woman appearing with a group of nine other twenty year olds, I would probably want to boo the eighty year woman off the show. After doing her dance it would be apparent that she didn't possess the same so-called qualities that we as a society would consider to be beautiful like the other nine contestants.

Her hair would more than likely be silver. Her face would probably have a few wrinkles. Her movements would be very slow and deliberate. She probably would have to stop and caught her breath every few minutes.

Now that I am much older and have traveled down a great many of life's roads the eighty year old woman would win the contest hands down. When one is older they come to understand that the beauty of life is found in the fact that one has endured. That eighty year old woman would have survived and weathered the many storms and still at her age, possessed the ability, grace and courage to compete with the much younger group.

At no time did she demonstrate any signs to indicate she was intimidated by the much younger contestants in the group. She did her thing by acting within the confines of her limitations. She made no attempts to impress the judges, just did her thing and when her act was over, she took her seat. No she didn't continue to stand like the others. That my friend is a thing of beauty.

Serious question, if you needed a second car in the family would you purchase one that is so old that it was about to fall apart or would you purchase one that you feel would be of a useful service to the family? I am not knocking the car because it is old but rather because it can serve no useful purpose to the family. In life there are seasons and everything and everybody are governed by seasons. If we use our given seasons wisely we can be as graceful and elegant as the eighty year old beauty contestant.

The point that I am attempting to make is if we continue to live we will get much, much older. Like in the beauty contest society doesn't view the eighty year old as having the same or anywhere near the marketability as the twenty year olds. Given this fact common sense should direct every young person to start thinking about their golden years. It would behoove a much younger person to come to the realization that contrary to their beliefs they will not remain young forever.

For each year that we age our marketability value depreciates. I know we are human and not houses, you go and tell that to the many seniors who are confined to homes. For the most part society has not done enough to ensure their continued comfort. The family that they the seniors are a part of may have had to put them in a home so they could continue with their own family.

Sadly, some of the seniors end up in homes because of their actions and conduct as youngsters. Switching from marriage to marriage and not taking the time to understand that they will need someone in their lives to be with as they get older. They failed to understand that their children may love them but their children will have their own lives to live. Now if the senior has money that is a different story.

Instead of trying to cultivate a meaningful union that will last them through the golden years for the most part each time a young couple has an argument or disagreement they are ready to take flight. Sure, while they are young and so-called marketable and pretty they will find someone else and begin to make them as miserable as they are. However, a very strange thing begins to happen each time they are in pursuit of a new partner it takes longer and longer to get one.

For you see nature has a way of tricking us or I should say that we have a way of tricking ourselves into believing that we will stay young and beautiful forever. Being the humans that we are when we are convinced by others that we are beautiful, we fail to continue to check the mirror for any changes. When you look at a ninety year old woman who may be wrinkled, do you think she was born that way. No she became that way over a number of years.

After the so-called young and beautiful person have used up their beauty and it is no longer with them especially since they can't find their new partner as quickly as before, they are the first to complain that they can't find themselves a good woman or man. Hell, they had nine or ten others and let them all go because they failed to invest in the cultivation of a good relationship. Didn't have the time. They knew that others wanted and desired them so they didn't have to put up with any bull—from anyone as they saw it.

So now that their marketability is near zero they now want to sit around and complain to others about how miserable their life is. Their friends and family really don't want to hear their complaints they are just being nice to them because they really don't want to hurt their feelings. For you see they know for a fact that they had at least two good partners and due to their failure to make them work they are where they are today. So they should just suck it up and go and try to prevent some other young so-called pretty person from making the same mistake by telling them the truth about life and how it works.

In our society the only thing old that people want is money. Now if you are old and just so happen to have money they will want you so they can gain access to your money. After the money is gone so are they. Had you been able to cultivate a meaningful union with your spouse while you were young you would have someone to at least talk to.

No instead, you paraded around like some proud peacock thinking you were all of that and a cup of diamonds. Now that you are old and alone, you want someone to feel sorry for you. Well I don't. It is almost like trying to trade in an old car with a million miles on it. Although you may think that the car still has value because you may know how it has served you in the past. Well in this society it is all about the young. When the dealer looks at the old car he or she will know that it is worthless so they will increase the price of the new car to offset the cost that they say they will give you for the old car. That is just an attempt to make you feel good about the situation. For as soon as the deal is made on the new car they will destroy the old as the junk that it really is.

Just to show you how some people don't think of the future and how things in life can happen. I will share an experience with you. Prior to my retirement, I had accrued nearly three thousand hours in sick leave. Now that in and of itself is really nothing to brag about.

It was that with the grace of God I didn't have any serious illnesses that kept me from going to work. Yes during those years I had ailments but just to say I had a headache and stay at home was not my way of thinking. I felt that if I was being paid to do a job it was my responsibility to carry out my end of the deal. In other words an honest day of work for an honest day of pay.

There was this one employee who would make fun of me for being so dedicated and devoted to my job. I would attempt to explain to the person that I was not necessarily devoted to the job but rather to myself and my family. The person didn't have a clue as to what I was talking about. If it was a nice and beautiful day the person would call in sick and go to the beach. It seemed as though that each time they earned any amount of leave they would use it.

The individual would tell me things like you could die tomorrow and all that leave would be wasted. I would reply by saying that I could also live tomorrow and something of which I had no control over could happen and I would be able to continue to get paid. That was so funny to them.

One day the word was circulate that the employee in question had been involved in a serious accident and it was estimated by the medical staff that it would require approximately six months for a total recovery. At the time of the accident, you guessed it, the employee didn't have any leave that would have enabled them to continue to receive a pay check.

When the circumstances of the employee's situation became known some of the employees started to collect money to ensure the employee received money to assist them in the time of their need. Additionally, where I worked there was a program in place wherein employees could contribute some of their accrued leave to other employees to assist them in times of need. The leave bank.

Being the human that I am when I was approached I had mixed feeling about donating my earned leave to the individual. I knew that my conscience would not allow me to just say no because I was not raised like that. My ambivalence was not about whether to give but rather how much to give. Make no mistake about it, it is sometimes difficult to support someone when they have knowingly thought of you as being a fool.

The struggle within myself didn't take too long. I contributed my leave to the individual as if they had never made fun of me. No big deal just glad that I could assist. Situations like that is tantamount to the judge telling the jury to forget what was said during a particular conversation during a court hearing. You just can't unring the bell.

If a married couple remains together for the long run the two of them would have the pleasure of talking about how they raised their children while they are sitting in the swing. For the most part that is just about all they will be able to do anyway but at least they will have each other. The two of them can look forward to seeing the grandkids as their children visit them during the summer. That is a joyous time and it also allows each member of the family to be cognizant of and appreciative of life's seasons.

Their grandchildren will being to see and feel the strenght in family and it will play a great role in their own personal developmental stages. Nothing on this earth can compare with the power of family. I am talking about a group of people that will stand with you whether you are right or wrong. Whether you are ugly or pretty. Whether you are rich or poor they stand better if you happen to have struck it rich. Nonetheless, they will be there for you.

In the end, if one fails to comport themselves in a manner in which nature has prescribed for us they are opening themselves up for a life of continued misery especially during their golden years. If one fails to understand and recognize the fact that in order to have a productive life as a senior citizen the appropriate seeds must be planted. One cannot wait until they are fifty plus years old and then attempt to find someone to be their companion. A relationship must be cultivated over the years.

Affairs

Visit any area in this country and you will hear of talk about crime. All areas may not be as bad as others but it does exist everywhere. Visit any town or area in this country and you will hear of talk about someone having or who have had an affair. Some folks will readily admit that having an affair is necessary for the preservation of their marriage. Others may have an affair because they have never been able to eradicate that thrill of the chase moment from their personality.

In some cases an individual's self-esteem may be so low that another person is needed to validate their mere existence. They must constantly have someone telling them how beautiful they are. You know, in the same manner in which they were told those things during the chase. If the husband or wife fails to continue with that type of behavior their partner will find it elsewhere.

That is one of the reasons that it is so important to be in love with yourself first. When one is in love with self they will know what it is like to be loved by others. In order to recognize love one must know what love is. Love is not allowing another human being to abuse you. Love is not taking advantage of others simpily because someone may like you.

Some will even tell you that having an affair is tantamount to having a spare tire in the event the marriage is blown up. Some even have affairs to gain material things and social advancement. No matter the reasons I can think of no scenario wherein any of the reasons put forth would be justified. Lets just state the real truth people have affairs because they are just whores who refuse to challenge themselves in the matter of being committed to themselves. Most importantly they don't love themselves.

If you will note I did not say refuse to be committed to someone else. I said refuse to be committed to themselves. When an individual is having a secret affair the other partner has no knowledge of the situation. Just like anyone who sits around and eat all the wrong foods and then attempts to blame others for being overweight. One cannot have an affair and then blame the spouse.

Each and everyone of us must be held accountable for our own actions. If my spouse likes to cook cakes and I allow myself to sit there and gorge myself on the cakes I cannot then blame my spouse for getting me fat. My fatness came about as a consequence of my own conduct not hers. Likewise, if your spouse cheats that doesn't give you the right or justification to go out and cheat. You know right from wrong and if the situation has gotten to the point that cheating is necessary the person just maybe telling you that you are no longer the object of their affections. Just maintain your diginity and do not allow yourself to be dragged down to that level.

I must tell you this story however, I don't really know all the facts. There was this guy who by society's standards was very handsome. He was a known player with all the women. One woman was never enough for him. He always thought he had to have two or three different women on the side. Chasing women was his primary game. Although married he would pursue women just for the sport of it. He was very charismatic and knew all the right things to say that would be of interest to most women.

Over the years so many married women have fallen prey to this guy because he is constantly on the prowl to trick or deceive some unsuspecting woman, especially a woman who is in the mist of a dispute with her husband. When that married woman happens to come in contact with this guy she can kiss her marriage goodbye. This guy will say all the right things and being in a vulnerable state she will gobble up his every word as if his words were the truth.

While guys like this exist the same can be said of women. For there was this woman who by society's standard was very beautiful, albeit nature was slowly extracting said beauty away. You must however give her credit for some years now she recognized some of the errors of her ways relative to men. Although she was getting older she was determined to find and capture that one man that she intended to spend the rest of her life with. She was every bit the chaser as the guy.

She had heard of this guy and had even seen him at a social event and from that day forward she was intent on getting him no matter the cost. During her much younger days while she was the dream of almost every guy that she met she had gone through enough wealthy men to acquire a small fortune. However, as time passed she started to realize that there was more to life than just pursuing money. She for at least one time in her life wanted to pursue or chase someone that she actually wanted other than for money.

What a pair they deserve each other. She had studied this guy and knew of all his likes and dislikes, his most profound like was trying to trick women, especially if he thought they had a little money. One night she purposely visited a place that she knew he frequented so she could engage him in a conversation.

When they met she told him that she was looking to hire a man to handle all of her finances because she had to devote her time and energy to another project she was working on. She told him that he would be paid well and the job came with many benefits. He accepted. She arranged it so he would have an overview of her finances. He was surprised to know that she was worth millions.

She was always very generous with him. Giving him hugh monthly bonuses. However, for the life of him he couldn't figure out what was happening in the situation. He knew that the job he was so called doing wasn't worth the amount of money being given to him. Being the player that he was he wondered if this women was setting him up to extract some sort of revenge for hurting one of her relatives.

He knew that she was older than himself. He also recognized the fact that she was a beautiful woman and he dared not say or do anything that would jeapordize him new found financial cash cow. He figured that he would bide his time until he was able to discern the game she was playing.

Like I said I didn't get the full story but it is my understanding that they did in fact get together. However, their relationship ended in tragedy. What else would one expect from a union of this nature. Everyone just playing a game purely for total selfish reasons. Albeit we are all selfish to a certain extent some are more so than others.

There are countless stories that can be told wherein people have been tricked into believing that they were the object of someone's affection when all the while they were just simply being used. We often hear of stories that involves real live criminals and not only the law enforcement personnel who are supposed to supervisor them, but lawyers and other so-called intelligent people falling prey to the words being spoken by the criminals. Married lawyers have even assisted in the actual escape of some criminals.

What would motivate a married lawyer to carry on an affair with an inmate that is actually locked behind prison walls with no hope of a good future? What is it the chase maybe, then again what chase? Maybe that is it, they didn't have to chase because he has already been captured. Knowing the individual is locked up and has no control he is totally dependent upon her for his freedom. Just maybe her husband wasn't as attentive and that side of her ego is being satisfied and she likes it and wants more or it.

Now I am no psychologist but I will venture to say that by helping the criminal to escape somewhere in the back of her mind she has convinced herself that the criminal will be just as totally devoted to her for helping him to escape as he was doing his incarceration. So sad and most times relationships of this nature end in tragedy.

There are untold stories wherein married men as well as women have actually left home to be with their supposedy lover only to find the person was only interested in their money or sex or for whatever reason they could use them for. A many a man as well as a many a woman have left their family and children just because the grass appeared to be much greener on the other side.

If a man or wowan has an affair with someone in hopes of someday getting together with that person what makes them think the person will ever trust them with having the knowledge that they cheated on their spouse with them. There would be no trust and even if one wanted to go to the corner store to get a newspaper suspicions would be abound. The person may not say anything at that moment but you can rest assured that a little light will go off that will remind them of the fact that they use to meet in that same manner.

It doesn't get better once the suspicion is arosed, the entire relationship become nothing but a spy game. One entire life is centered around trying to listen to one end of a conversation when their spouse is on the phone. Always listening for some key word or phrase. Always listening for some secret pass code. Who want to live like that. The **stress** of a situation like this will surely cause this union to end.

To get a better understanding of the word affair lets just call it what it is. For the most part an affair is nothing more than free sex without the responsibility of commitment. Most guys or gals who have married partners will clearly tell you that as long as their cheating partner remains with their spouse the relationship can continue. If talk ever occurs about the possibility of their lover leaving their spouse the relationship will end sooner rather than later.

It wasn't about love but rather free sex and if the married person does something to piss the lover off the lover just may tell the spouse just to get a measure of revenge. One needs to be free to live life at it's fullest. With shadows like that hanging over one's head it is difficult to relax. If the married person has had some disagreement with the lover each time the phone rings the person nerves are on edge. The unsuspecting spouse in this case will not have to conduct any investigation because in due time the **stress** of the situation will force the cheating spouse to give themselves away.

There goes the marriage and the person that they were cheating with will want nothing to do with them. The husband or wife will no longer be able to trust the cheating spouse even if they make an attempt to reconcile or patch up their differences because the trust factor will be missing for sometime to come.

A relationship can work however if the two people are truly serious about making it work. However, it will take years and years to regain the missing trust.

Even then the cheating partner must understand that their partner has every right to be suspicious of their every move. As such, if they want to save the union they must commit themselves to the rigor and **stress** that will surely be present in their everyday lives. Sometimes the **stress** of trying to prove to their spouse that they will no longer cheat is too much to overcome and they sometimes have to end the relationship.

Stress

Throughout this book the word **stress** is continually found. Given this fact it is safe to conclude that **stress** is an integral factor in the overall deterioration of a marriage. When anyone is under **stress** they will do and act in ways that are not normal for them as I stated earlier. They will be taken out of their safe bodily element.

Take for example a solider confined to a war zone in which his/her life is constantly under the threat of being taken. The constant noise of the guns sounding or mortar shells exploding all around them will eventually have a deleterious effect. For a young person this maybe a fun and thrilling thing for a while but eventually the overall constant threat of death becomes a reality. Somewhere maybe not necessarily on the battle field those **stressful** moments will have a negative impact on the overall stability of the solider.

I am a Viet Nam veteran who was ordered there by my country in the sixties still more than forty years later I am still fighting the Viet Nam war in my head and I suffers from PTSD. I can't recall the last time that I received a good night sleep without being drunk. Although I stopped drinking some years ago because I could see the negative affect the drinking was having on my family. Still, I wake up every night in the middle of the night from some nightmare about the war or about some other scary event.

I often tell people that I do not have to spend my money going to see a scary movie show because I view one every night for free. I will be honest with you I do not consider myself to be a good writer or even an average writer. I write because when I awake in the middle of the night it gives me something to do with my time. I feel that anyone over the age of fifty-five or maybe even younger has a book or two in them. Their life experiences surely makes them eligible to talk about some of the things that they have encountered.

I was always told that words of wisdom can come from a fool if said words are factual and useful. Why am I talking about my military experiences you might ask? The breakup of so many marriages gives us all a very good reason to be concerned. My concern is the safety and stability of the children. So if I can say anything to help in that regard I will continue to do so.

In order to bring this **stress** message and the impact it has on marriages closer home it is appropriate to clearly define the word. This is how I define the word. Being placed or put in a situation or condition that forces one to endure all aspects of said condition when in fact the body and mind clearly knows that it has been taken out of it's normal pattern or element. When the body, anyone's body and mind is forced to conduct business or operate beyond the scope of it's limitations the body and mind may do anything in an attempt to get itself back to what is normal for it.

In my case, the constant gun fire and mortar attacks were too much for my mind and body, so in an attempt to get relief I started using alcohol and drugs. My body and mind were experiencing and seeing things that it was not accustomed to seeing and it needed a way to escape. Now you may say that the drugs and alcohol scenario is tantamount to the person overeating. Well, I can't argue the point because you just maybe right.

However, with the overeating situation one is aware certain illnesses and even death may occur over a period of time. That time will not usually happen at any moments notice as with the solider fighting in a combat zone. In that case the constant threat of death is forever present. I will not speak for others but I chose to keep myself high to deal with the **stress** of the constant threat of death. I am in no way attempting to justify my actions just stating the facts on how **stress** affected me. You know, the truth will set you free type thing.

As I said earlier in a marriage two people are expected to come together and become one. Seriously think about that for a moment. I am certain you must agree that it just doesn't make any sense. When couples try to actually make or force it to happen the only results that can be attained is unwanted **stress** and that is no good for any of us.

In my own personal opinion I honestly believe that **stress** related incidents are the leading cause of deaths in this country. Take a drunk driver for instance he or she is attempting to force his or her body to control itself after consuming excessive amounts of alcohol. Moreover, when one is under continued **stress** it forces the body to shut down and not function properly. For example, if one puts oil in the gasoline tank of a vehicle they can expect for it not to operate properly.

Same with the body and mind if it is constantly exposed to situations that it deems to be inappropriate for the continued safe operation of itself it will start to shut down in other areas. That's just maybe one of the many reasons you have learned individuals doing so many things that you wouldn't normally expect them to do. In order for the body to adjust to unwanted situations I am convinced that it may draw strength from other sections of the body to protect the area that is in need of protecting.

Leaving for example the area that cover the control of headache susceptible to the headache. At this point while reading, I know you must concluded that I spent too much time in Viet Nam talking like that. Let me say this, we all have our own little ways of dealing with the things that affects our daily lives. No, I am not a doctor but from my personal experiences that is how **stress** seems to affect me. When I am **stressed** out I may get a headache or stomachache and other parts of my body seem to be affected.

If my spouse nags me or I nag her everyday about something that she or I have done be it something big or small eventually it will start to take a serious toll on the marriage. You will get to the place that you just want to avoid your partner. Just stay clear of them because you just don't want to hear the noise. The constant nagging can cause one to have nightmares. Even when one is asleep one will be awaken in the middle of the night hearing that loud and screaming voice. This can have serious consequences.

The sad thing about a nagger is the fact that they never ever take the time to evaluate themselves. Whatever they do they seem to think that they are perfect and only if the world would adhere to their way of thinking we would have a perfect society. They fail to realize that the constant nagging by them is a clear sign that something just maybe wrong with them. Why is it they reason that no other human being on this earth can do any thing right? They have all the answers for everything and everybody.

If you will notice a nagger can always find fault with others or put others down for the way a person may conduct themselves. When in reality if the nagger only took a moment to think about it they would actually see that they don't really love themselves. For if they did they would attempt to find ways to enjoy most of the things they did in life instead of talking about or finding fault with everybody else.

In order words if I like to listen to music and you don't like it, don't put me down for liking music. For you see I could put you down for not liking music. Just a matter of preference and we must be bold enough to allow each other to exist in our own private domain. I don't really expect you to derive pleasure from most of the things that I do just like I am certain that I will not derive pleasure from most of the things that you do.

Nonetheless, I will defend your right to enjoy yourself in our home. That is one of the main reasons that it is essential that we have and maintain our own private space within our home. If you don't like my music stay out the room.

Everyone must have a private place. Since I don't like your makeup taking up all the space in the bathroom I will use my own bathroom, etc. etc.

When the guys come over to watch a sporting event we will confine ourselves to a specific area. After all you should be extremely proud of the fact that I enjoy spending my time at home instead of the streets. I know of a lot of guys who spend a great deal of time in the streets away from home and some of the time spent out is not all work related.

So woman please don't **stress** me out for every little thing that I do. For you see I am only human. Moreover, it is you with the problem not me. On a daily basis I make an attempt to afford you the opportunity to conduct yourself in a manner that will ensure your happiness. I don't nag you about every little thing that you do that doesn't please me. I just suck it up an make an attempt to be happy. Not you, you must call me on every little thing that I do and I am getting **stressed** out and may have to move soon.

I must therefore ask you are you happy with your life? If not, I strongly suggest you make some changes when it comes to your habit of attempting to correct everything that I do. Otherwise, for the safety of both of us I just may be out of here. For you see I can no longer take the **stress** that you are forcing my body and mind to endure. All of my energy is being used in an attempt to stay sane.

You seem to want to challenge each and everything that I do. You tell me that I don't squeeze the tooth paste properly. When I ask you what is the proper way you just tell me that your way is the way that everyone else does it. When I ask you for data to prove your assertion you tell me that I am crazy. When I ask you to show me the proper way of squeezing tooth paste as listed or specified in the Tooth Paste police manual so the tooth paste police want arrest me, you tell me that there is no such manual. Then the next logical question is what make you think that the way you squeeze it is the correct and proper way? Moreover, I don't give a damn how others conduct their own personal business. They must do what they think is right for themselves and I must do what is best for me.

The simple fact of the matter is you are accustomed to squeezing it a certain way and since we live in the same house, you want me to do it your way. Well I am not going to do it your way, because I too am use to doing it my way and will continue to do so. In order to maintain peace in our household we can agree to own and purchase our own tooth paste and that will resolve that issue.

You tell me that I snore too loudly. Now you know that I have gone to the doctor in an attempt to get this problem under control. Yet, you continue to nag me. The doctor told me that to lose ten or twenty pounds may help. You know I am trying to work on that. However, due to your constant nagging I am unable to put all of my focus on the things in my life that are important. You tell me that I like to snore loudly just to get on your nerves or to just plain make your life a living hell. How absurd, do you think I like living like this? The solution for this is we will have separate bedroom and that way I can snore with a clear head.

You tell me that I put my friend's interest ahead of yours'. Well let me tell you something, when I am around my friends they treat me as an equal and at no time do they attempt to make me think that I am stupid and don't know how to handle any of life's situations. Everytime we attempt to carry on a conversation I can't get a word in edgewise because you must give out the law like Moses did and if I fail to listen you seem to think that I am being disobedient. First of all, you need to understand that I am not your child.

You tell me that I fail to lower the toilet seat after usage. Let me explain something to you. When I lifted the seat up in the first place it was with you in mind. Had I failed to lift it prior to using it there was a good possibility that water would be inadvertently sprayed on it during my usage.

Now I must ask you is it better for you to lower a dry toilet seat or be subjected to using a possibly wet one? So I forgot to lower the seat you should be happy that I had the kind thought of thinking of your well being prior to my usage. I tell you what from now on we will use separate bathrooms. That way I can lift or not lift the seat and most importantly, I will not have to deal with the **stress** of the situation.

When I attempt to show you that I care for you, you tell me that I smother you with so much attention. When I back off and attempt to spend more time with my friends, you tell me that I ignore you. Which is it? For you see I will not be torn in your indecisiveness. I tell you what from now on I will do it my way. The **stress** of going back and forth is killing me and I will no longer do it like that.

It appears that you expect me to jump through hoops every time you say something. Not only that no matter what I am doing you expect me stop at that moment and obey your command. I get no respect and I am getting tired of it. You constantly complain to your family and friends about how lazy or no good I am while all the time we are never behind on any of our bills. You are just one of those people that will never be happy. Your happiness is derived from criticizing the so-called shortcomings of others, get a grip.

You tell me that my shoes should be placed in a certain area of the house. What kind of king of my castle am I if I can't do some of the most simple things that I like. It is of great comfort to me to know that my shoes are in a certain place and not someplace where you have placed them without my knowledge or approval. When I need most any of my personal items I need to hire a blood-hound to track them down because your main concern is how things may look to others in the house.

I can understand your concern relative to visitors seeing the living room, family room and maybe certain other areas. Your control of me and where I place my personal items extend well beyond those boundaries. You even attempt to control my hobby area. I thought when we married that I would have a place within our home to express my individuality. Listening to you and all the things that you demand of me it appears that you are some warden running a prison and I must comply with your demands or be punished.

I am not that concerned about what visitors may say when they come to our home after all, they pay no mortgage note nor any other bills that must be paid. I am more concerned with me having a place wherein I can be delivered from the tolls of a hard days work. A place that I can unwind without the fear of someone looking over my shoulder telling me that I am doing something wrong. I had enough of that type treatment while at work.

So what if I am doing something wrong in my own home that I thought I shared with someone who would allow me to be me. I do not need the same pressure at home that I encounter in the work place and in the general public. While at work if I make a mistake I am subject to be fired or demoted. While in the general public I am subject to be robbed, mugged, run over by a speeding motorist, or just cursed out because someone is having a bad day. I can understand it if a burglar breaks into our home and make demands. You are worst than the burglar because your demands never stops.

With all the commands and demands that you are making of me it maybe more beneficial for me to just stay at work at least I am being paid for being abused.

The only thing that you offer relative to compensation is more abuse on top of the abuse that you have already given out. You don't even offer any benefits for taking your abuse and you expect me to like and except it.

Religious Beliefs

Inasmuch as my spouse and I had successfully raised our children to adulthood we decided that it would be in our best financial interest to relocate to a much smaller town. One day while canvassing the general area for a church to attend I saw one and pointed it out to the spouse. She immediately stated that she wouldn't want to attend that one because it appeared to be of a particular denomination (which I will not mention, because everyone has the right to attend the church of their choice).

For some strange reason I wanted to follow-up on that comment. So I asked are you saying that when we move to heaven that we will be afforded the opportunity to travel around in an attempt to find the church or people of our choice? I thought we would all be as one in heaven. I asked if there would be different denominations in heaven and if so, how would I know which one would be right for me? Of course I didn't get an answer to any of my questions.

When it comes to going to heaven I really don't know what the people on earth will do. The most segregated day of the week is Sunday. If I happen to visit your church impromptu and decide that your church is not right for me I just may bash your method of worship and may even call the members heathens and condemn them to hell for not believing as I do. What I really should be doing is making an attempt to understand you and you should be doing likewise.

As I understand it there is only one heaven. Now if that is really the case it appears to me that religious leaders should reach out to all other churches in an attempt to understand, tolerate and accept each other. Each church should set aside certain days for people of different denominations to attend their services and totally embrace them with open arms.

Then again I don't think that can ever happen because confusion about the money would become an issue. That's right, the money. It is all about the money. Churches would not want to take the chance of exposing members to other services because they just may lose a few members to the other church. In that regard I must therefore ask myself is the saving of souls or the collection of money the most important factor?

If you notice in our society some religious belivers will actually tell you that you are going to hell if you fail to worship as they prescribe. Sad part about that is they really believe that. Some may even attempt to cast evil spirits on you. When a person of this nature approaches me I immediately recognize the so-call evil spirit, the evil spirit is them.

Nonetheless, some people I should say that many people have fallen prey to people who purports to know God personally. One must be very careful in listening to people when religion is being discussed. Know thy self first. Know what is right for you first. Know that you have people in this world who will take advantage of you in the name of God.

For the most part our individual religious beliefs were handed down from our parents or grandparents. Which in my opinion, doesn't make any of us right about anything. It only makes us right from our varing perspective. So when the spouse attempts to save my soul from hell's damnation I just ask her why has she stayed with me all these years if I am so evil. Would she not be an accessory to evil and not allowed into heaven if she knowingly stayed with me knowing that I was evil? For the most part most people are just confused from all the things that they are told about religion starting from the time that they were still children.

So the real question is when two people come together in a marriage union what is the correct faith to follow? Inasmuch as we all have differing opinions I personally say the one that will be of most benefit to you, the individual. One should feel free to pursue their own personal religious beliefs and both parties should be tolerant and respectable of the other's belief. Don't attempt to save me into heaven save yourself.

If we all raise our children to **do unto all others as they would have others do unto them,** irrespective of religion we would all be able to live our lives in peace. For you see if I respect you and you respect me we will clearly be able to understand the true value of life. If you scrutinize history you will find that more people have died in the name of religion than from any other source. Think about it.

Just like a family trying to live in one house under the same roof we must all live in this world under the same sky. If we are to live in peace, just like the marriage as many **stress** related factors must be eliminated. If you want to start a quick argument start a conversation about politics or religion.

Children should be allowed to be children. Allow them to explore and acquire all the knowledge they can relative to the natural things in life. When a child becomes an adult if said child has been equipped and taught the basic fundamentals regarding life they will be able to discern what is right and proper for them relative to their religious beliefs. Moreover, religion can't be taught it must be felt by the individual and you cannot force me to feel a certain way. If you attempt to force me I will pretend that I believe you just to keep you out of my personal space.

You can tell me every story that was ever written by religious scholars and if I can't comprehend the meaning of what you are saying from my intellectual reasoning you are wasting your time. Teach your child how to count so others want cheat him or her out of their money. Teach your child to be respectful of the elderly. Inasmuch as we must all live on this planet teach your child not to be so selfish and to share with other.

Teach your child about the fragilities of the human character. Teach them that it is okay to fall down as long as they make an attempt to get back up. Teach them that nothing in life is perfect not even their parents. Many children becomes disillusioned with life when they discover that life as mom and dad explained it does not exist.

We must forever be cognizant of the fact that there are those among us who will concoct a scheme to justify their evil deeds. Some will even cheat on their spouse and invoke the name of God. If you listen to them long enough they will convince you that God actually sent the person in their live to rescue them from the horrible person that they are married to.

They will actually attempt to convince you that they had a talk personally with God and he instructed them to follow the destructive course of action that they have embarked upon. The really, really sad part about this conduct is they may actually believe what they are saying. If they actually believe what they are saying you are dealing with one dangerous person.

They will do anything to you or anyone else who attempts to stand in their way because to them they have God's blessings. If you attempt to challenge what they are saying they will condemn you to hell. Your children will become so torn that it will take years and years of counseling to get them to be anywhere normal. Even though most everyone else will recognize them for the basket case that they are the children will have suffered the most.

You Don't Own Me

In the early years of our society women and wives were actually so-called owned by men and they were viewed as personal property. Just like with any custom or tradition that has been allowed to continue over a great number of years it is difficult to change that mindset. Throughout it all women have prevailed and are now considered to be on equal par with the men. It should be noted however, that the salary gap is still not equal that is another book in and of itself.

During a period in our society women were just housewives who oversaw the smooth operation of the physical home while the man was considered the overall bread winner and was required to just ensure all the physical needs outside of the home were taken care of. Each had their own personal duties and it was acceptable. Then something strange started to happen the man could no longer support the family on his salary alone.

At that point it became increasingly necessary for the wife to work outside of the home. Although many men didn't like the idea common sense told him that he had no other choice other than to accept it. When the women started to make money many men viewed that as a threat to their manhood. Some even left the family because they felt as though they were less than a man for not being able to provide for their family. Ego. With the man having the mindset that he must care for his family it can be understood that he reasoned that he was in charge of his wife.

His abandonment of the family is a clear indication that he felt that he had lost total control. As time passed the ole boy realized that women and men were put on this earth to be with each other. So the ole boy had to put his pride aside and make an attempt to adjust to the changing world. Begrudgingly, he went back home to be with his family because he simply missed them.

However, in the back of his mind he couldn't allow the wife to outdo him and he would ensure she stayed in her place. After all, he was still the man of the house and he would ensure it stayed that way. Let the games begin again.

When it became apparent that the woman would not be able to do all the physical things in the household prior to going to work. The man became resentful. In his mind it was still the responsibility of the woman to handle all the household duties irrespective of her outside the home obligations. This became a very serious issue and even to his very day it is very much a serious issue in many homes.

Some men just cannot get it through their heads that they may have to wash the cloths, change the diapers, cook dinner, help with the children's homework and perform many other tasks around the house. Some homes however are very enlighten, the husband may have become the house person because the wife's salary is much more than that of the husband. These homes have come to know the importance of survival and understand that it takes team work to survive.

The man with his head stuck in the sand who refuses to fully except change is forever attempting to find ways and schemes to control his spouse. He must have the final say because that is the way he was raised. The man of the house must have the final say. If he can't be in control as viewed by him and his fellow peers with that mindset they are viewed as wimps. They are not necessarily concerned with the smooth operation of the household they must have the final word.

Which by the way only serves to add undue **stress** on the wife because she maybe earning just as much or more in salary as he is. Instead of being concerned about the overall operation of the family he is more concerned with him manhood. When the wife attempt to discuss this issue with him he can't really find a way to justify his actions so he proclaims that he doesn't want to talk about it. His inner self is in so much conflict that it is difficult for him to function in an orderly manner.

He really needs some serious counseling. He never stops to think of the impact his behavior maybe having on his son and how that impact may cause his son to treat women in the future. Believe me the son is watching and will someday take his place in society. Like the father he will be forever consumed with the thought that men must be above women.

At some point in the relationship the wife will explode. She has to. The **stress** of the situation is just too great for her to continue living like this. In some homes this conduct probably would have played out like this. While she is making a meaningful attempt to keep the family together this jerk is acting like a small brat who just wants to have his way. She has suggested counseling and that suggestion was met with negative results.

She even suspects that he has taken up drinking. One day he comes home rambling about how he is not getting any respect in him own home and he is getting sick and tired of it. Well, for her this was it since it was a Saturday night and neither of them had to report for work the next day, she would wait until the next day when his mind is clear and have it out with him.

It was a beautiful day and she dreaded what she had to do but do it she must. She decided that she would be as honest and forthright as possible put all of her cards on the table. She knew that she would not stand idly by and allow her husband to ruin not only her life but also the lives of their children.

She may have started out by saying I love you and would very much like to keep this family together. He instantly becomes offended. Are you threatening to leave me. She just flatly said yes, that is if your attitude doesn't change. That was the end of that conversation he stormed out the door heading for his car. She had no regret because she knew she had to do what she did.

While driving away he is thinking of all sorts of unsavory names that fits the description of her. His mind kept going back to the day that he had heard of where men could actually beat their women and get away with it. The day that men actually owned their women. He knew that he couldn't allow himself to be controlled by a woman. He figured that he would stay away from home for a few days and return home and she would be glad to see him. That would be her punishment for disrespecting him.

When he returned home the wife and children were no where to be found. He then drove to her parents home. When he knocked on the door the father answered it and informed him that yes, they were there, however they did not want to see him at this time. Futhermore, the father informed him that he was no longer welcomed at his home at this time and that his daughter will call him later via cell phone to make arrangements for him to see his children.

In her mind it was over she was done with the disrespect. She knew that she had to move on with her life.

That scenario could happen in any marriage. People who are not willing to break from old customs and taboos like the husband may just find themselves forced out of a meaningful relationship. Inasmuch as so many elements and ingredients are involved in making a marriage work it would behoove a couple to be open minded when it comes to preserving the union for a long period of time.

Men as well as women must come to the realization that they are equal partners and no one owns the other. They must identify their priorities and chart a rational course of action to achieve them. I can't tell my spouse that this is the way my parents did a certain thing because that method may on longer be relevant in today's society.

If you or your spouse enjoys reading or watching television during the late hours of the night do not attempt to change that just because the light or noise may affect you. Go to another room. You should be in your own bedroom anyway. For if you were in your own bedroom you wouldn't have to worry about that in the first place.

A person **MUST** be able to enjoy a few of life's simple pleasures while in their own home. Otherwise, it would be totally futile to invest so much time, money and effort. Both partners **Must** work toward achieving that objective. If after a hard day's work I can't come to my house and relax, I may as well take the money that I am paying for the mortgage and toss it down the sewer. It really serves no useful purpose for one to be misable all the time. Especially, when the one causing the misery is sleeping next to you.

The Selection Process

When the dog chases the vehicle it doesn't matter about the contents of the vehicle. Likewise, when some of us make an attempt to select a partner we take no time to look into what the person is all about. Man, did you see the body on her or girl he is the best looking man that I have ever seen. One must remember that some of the most deadliest things in life are beautiful and some of those things can kill you instantly.

Therefore, from a common sense perspective it would behoove one to acquire as much information and to know what it does before you start the chase. If during the chase you discover that it may be defective from your perspective call off the chase. Don't for one second convince yourself that you can fix or adjust the shortcomings to meet your specifications.

You know, I've got to have that at all cost even though he or she may not be just what you want. After all we reason we all have faults. If that little light goes off during the chase period you would be better served to clearly investigate all aspects of your concern. For just as sure as you are reading this there will come a time that you will wish that you had taken the time to look deeper.

One night of so-called good loving does not necessarily set the stage for a long and enduring marriage. Even though the individual may be so-called beautiful now imagine what they will look like ten to twenty years from now. For example, if you don't like big boned people (I will not call them fat) and even though your potential spouse is thin now you would be better served to visit his or her relatives and check them out. As they say, the apple doesn't fall to far from the tree.

Try to find a picture of the mother and father when they were about your potential spouse's age. If they were thin then and over the years due to metamorphosis, they have become somewhat obese you may want to stay away from that person.

If you marry the person clearly knowing that the mother and father is somewhat overweight don't complain later that your spouse has gained a lot of weight. Don't get me wrong, I am not against anyone its just that society has tricked most of us into believing that all of us must be thin. That will never happen anyway.

Ladies, if a man has a full head of hair when you meet him and you detest baldheaded men you know the score, better check out his father. More often than not if the father is now bald and he had a full head of hair at your potential spouse's age, you guessed it. You must also think of the children that you may have in the future. What will they look like.

I mention those things because some among us are vain like that. The fact of the matter is we should all come to the realization that we are all human beings and as such, will change during the course of our life time. If you love someone love them with the knowledge that one day they will not be able to do all the things or look the same way that the two of you did while you were young.

Know that one or both of you may become ill and one or the other may have to care for all of the needs of the other. With that in mind a union may just last. On the other hand, if one is selfish and think that the world revolves around them, the union is lost before it starts.

As I age I just laugh about it. First of all, inasmuch as I cannot control the aging process, I may as well attempt to find some humor in the process. All one has to do in order to get or acquire an understanding of life's process is look at their parents, their aunts and uncles and grandparents. As time passes they are actually looking at an accelerated view of themselves. Yes, the wrinkles, the silver hair, the stooped body.

Common sense should therefore behoove us to attempt to make as many friends as we can while we are younger because as we age we will need someone to just talk to and if one has been all about themselves it will not be pleasurable to be around them. Not too many people are interested in someone when all they talk about is themselves.

It Takes Time To Blossom

When a farmer plants a seed he or she is aware that it will take time in order to see any appreciable results. The farmer will visit the planted seed on a daily basis for he knows that he must be forever viligant if he intends to reap a meaningful harvest. From the very beginning the farmer knows that there are certain inherent things that he must watch for.

For example, if not kept in check weeds will stunt the growth of the seeds. Droughts or bad weather can become a factor. If the farmer fails to take the appropriate action relative to his crop all of his work would have been in vain. Like the farmer planting his seeds there are certain inherent dangers associated with marriage. Like the farmer, if the couple want good results it would behoove them to check to discern the status of the marriage on a regular basis. The greater the frequency the better for the marriage.

I recall during the course of raising my children I would sometimes sit them down and ask them if everything was alright in their lives. I told them that I didn't want them to wait until they were adults and recall some incident that adversely affected their lives. You know, for them to some day write a book pronouncing how they were mistreated by their parents. Although we would laugh about that I was very serious. The same must be done in a marriage. The partners must from time to time just sit and examine the status of the marriage. I will even take it a step further.

In everyday life we are required to renew our driver's license on an established basis. Why is that other than the fact that the state must find ways to extract money from all of us? A teacher may be required to renew his/her teaching certificate. A doctor may be required to renew his or her license. Well, inasmuch as children are involved in most marriages and since we pretend to care about the well being of our children, all marriage with children involved should be required to renew their marriage license on a recurring basis. Maybe once every four years or so.

If that was a mandatory requirement it would be difficult for couples to just take their marriage for granted. Most importantly, it would force them to at least think about the union and what they are suppose to mean to each other. I say that because in this society we must find ways to increase the importance of marriages. The raising of the children should take priority over all other things in our society. That is if we really want a sound nation.

If a child is raised in a dysfunctional family how in the world can he or she be expected to carry on or become a meaningful citizen in our society. If we continue to raise dysfunctional children the sum total will eventually be a dysfunctional nation. Therefore, it would behoove us as a nation to make an attempt to save our children. If renewing marriage licenses can stimulate our overall interest in marriages so be it.

Something is happening in this country and we had better take the time, energy and effort to determine what is going on. For the most part we fail to put our efforts where our mouth is. We in this country like to view things on some chart and say this is how things should work. Well, not even the charts are not doing too good now. Each time our so-called leaders come up with a plan that is intended to help society it seems to blow up in their faces.

More emphasis is being placed on the ownership of things and money rather than the interest of the children. It seems as though more money is being spent on exploring outer space than on within our earth's space. Even if we find that we can live on another planet what good will that knowledge do us if in fact we can't successfully live in peace on this one?

Who would the government take to the new planet anyway. I am certain that it wouldn't be the malcontents of our society. That leaves only the rich and powerful. The elitist. Yet, all of our tax dollars assist in paying for all those programs. To prove my point, just look at society today only the privileged are really enjoying the full impact of the American dream. Don't get me wrong, I am no fool I can't think of another country that I would rather be in. We must just view the situation as for what it really is.

Do you actually think that people with millions and millions of dollars have a need to worry about high fuel cost and all the other things that maybe pushing the average family into bankruptcy. Don't get me wrong, I am not against people having money but we must also be cognizant of the fact and the impact that the lack of money have on those in our society. If I don't have any bread or milk to feed my kids and I see you with those things, I am going to do all that I can to get some of what you have by any means necessary. My actions against you would not be based on any personal dislike for you but rather out of survival.

Instead of the government investing so much money in the outer space program more of it should be invested on inner earth space programs. Allow more tax breaks for working families with children. Give those families more of an incentive to remain together. When a family is burden down with financial issues it creates undue **stress** and we all know the results of that.

Inasmuch as we proclaim that the children are our most important asset and that they are the future of our country structure the laws so that a married couple can see a real appreciable difference if they remain married. You might ask what if it is a bad marriage? For the most part a bad marriage come about as a result of undue **stress**. What is more **stressful** on a marriage than the lack of money to buy the most simple basic needs. In many lower and middle-class homes when the family thinks that they have found a little breathing room the gas prices or some other necessary item for survival increases. On a daily basis it becomes more and more difficult for the average family to make it.

If one is wealthy the cost of things has no affect on them. What about the family that is struggling from pay check to pay check with no hope in sight. Don't kid yourself you can bet this has an adverse impact on those families. We must therefore ask ourselves what kind of seeds are we planting and most importantly, are we taking the proper care to ensure said seeds will be free to flourish?

Are we attempting to remove as many imperilments as possible? Are we keeping watch to ensure the weeds doesn't over run or stunt the growth of our planted seeds? Are we keeping watch on our seeds to ensure they are properly nurtured while they are young or are we so consumed with pursuing the all mighty dollar that no one has the time to check on the crop?

Time has proven over and over again that for the most part when a child is not properly raised he/she will become a burden on society. A child if not led in the right direction will more than likely gravitate toward all the wrong things in our society.

When no one is properly watching the crop after it is planted there will come a time when we finally get around to revisiting it, due to our negligence we will not recognize it. We will then stand there and pretend to be shocked. What did you expect? Did you really think that you could just plant some seeds and they would just flourish just because you planted them? Wrong, it doesn't work that way. Talk about not being able to see the forest for the trees, in this particular case you will not be able to see the plants for the weeds.

When we hear of all the trouble that our youth are encountering today, the rich as well as the poor does it give us pause to think maybe something is going wrong? No, because we somehow think the problems will solve themselves. Just like the seeds that we failed to nurture the same thing will happen to our children. Although we knew that droughts were confronting us, we never took the time to even make an attempt to water the seeds because it would have taken time away from some of our other so-called important endeavors.

Maybe it is me maybe I am missing something. Will someone, anyone, please tell me how mom and dad can nurture their children when it is a constant battle between the two them on who is the most important and God's gift to the world? They are so consumed with the style of their house, car or bank account that the children comes in after all of those things are factored in.

Some parents will know prior to going to work that their child is ill, yet they will still go because they have a deadline that must be met. Don't get me wrong I understand the importance of meeting a deadline but which of the two is more important. When a child is crying for the parents due to illness and the parent just abandons the child for whatever reason the child will carry that feeling for the rest of their life. The child must know that their security blanket is always there.

Speaking of deadlines some among us in society will sometime think that the job is the most important thing in life. I know that I talked earlier about the importance of going to work and that is true. However, one's work habits should be centered around the needs of the family and not some frivolous personal pleasure trip. In other words if a person went to work on a regular basis if an emergency arose at home everyone would understand that the employee must be telling the truth and would do everything to assist him or her.

On the other hand, the employee with the abysmal leave record just maybe questioned extensively regarding their request for emergency leave. That person never took the time to understand the importance of family. It was all about them and some pleasure situation. A great deal of people among us have no problem in attempting to lend a helping hand if it appears that the person is attempting to help themselves.

The little seeds are being stunted by the weeds because the parents failed to take the time to ensure proper cultivation. When it dawns on the parents that they should have taken the time to ensure the field was properly cultivated it just may be too late. They will then stand up and say that they were great parents. I guess they may feel that way because of the expensive house thay may live in or the expensive car they may drive. Success to them did not translate into raising their children successfully to adulthood.

Success meant out dueling their neighbors. Success meant sending the children to the most expensive schools without the proper input from themselves. In the end these type of parents will someday wish that they had taken more time and better care of their children. For as we age we will clearly begin to see the importance of our children. If we live long enough there will come a time in our lives that just to sit and hear our grown children voices will be a needed blessing. We will marvel at how that small seed has grown into a wonderful human being.

On the other hand if the children are somewhere spaced out in never-never land due to the negligence of the parents the parents will have no one to blame but themselves. Those parents as they age would be willing to give most of their expensive material things if they had some grandchildren to visit with them. As they age they begin to see the true value of life. As they age and become lonelier they will know that they made some very wrong decisions in their younger years.

Young folks, don't let all of those things happen to you. Take the time while you are young to cultivate lasting relationships. Take the needed time to ensure you raise your children properly. I will even say that it is okay to be selfish but if you are, just don't have any children because they will need your undivided attention.

One of the most important things that parents can give to their children is love. In a child's life there is no greater power. If parents shower their children with love that love will transfer itself to the making of the grandchildren. For if your child was loved and knows love said child will also love his or her own children. That to me seems to be a good investment in the making of a stable nation. If the families within a nation are sound so is the nation.

On the other hand, if we do nothing to properly ensure that our children are raised in caring and loving families we really want have to worry about some foreign country invading us with the intent to destroy us. For due to our negligence our seeds would not have had the proper care and will therefore wither from within.

As great as this nation is, the biggest threat as with the Romans and so many other cultures comes from within. You have politician lying to the public just to be elected. You have some ministers sleeping with some of the congregation members or lusting in their hearts for them. The people in power just tell us to keep the faith and don't worry because everything will be alright.

However, what they are really saying is as long as we rich folks can keep you in your place we can remain on top. They realize that they don't want too many people to become rich like them because if that ever came about the rich would have no one to do their dirty work. Can you imagine seeing a rich and wealthy man or woman cleaning out the local sewer. The wealthy will always need someone to look down on and to do their dirty work otherwise, their ascension to power would be rather useless.

There is only so much room for the elite in any given society and if one can't pass the cruelty test one need not apply. In this country there is this constant debate about the tax cuts for the wealthy come on now who makes the laws in the first place? I don't see any poor people in a position to make any laws. Even if one was knowledgable enough to somehow get into such a position due to his or her lack of money and influence they would be drowned out by the rich and power-ful folks.

Yet when it comes time for the country to be defended mostly the poor and underprivileged serve as the foot soldiers while the elite serve as the officers or general staff. When the little foot soldier returns home from the war all broken or maimed the bureaucracy or the elite may just push him or her aside for what they may consider to be more important and pressing issues or matters.

If we as a nation gets nothing else in this country right we should focus all of our energy on the overall better development of all of our children. We can either attempt to ensure that they are properly cared for while they are youug or we can wait later when they come unmanageable. Pay, we will one way or the other.

Imagine a young handsome man in his early twenties approaching an attrac-tive young lady in her early twenties and saying that he would like to marry her so the two of them could get old together. Firtst of all, that would be the end of that conversation because the dreaded word old would have been injected into the conversation. A young person hearing the word old in that context would be tan-tamount to someone yelling fire in a movie theater.

A young person never wants to hear the word old or be associated with it rela-tive to their private life. Sure, they may visit with their much older grandparents but at the age of twenty something they cannot for the life of themselves envision themselves being the future grandparents. For you see they have every intention of staying young forever. The young folks fail to understand that it is all a part of the blossoming process.

The most important thing that they fail to grasp is the fact that if a relation-ship is not properly cultivated from the very beginning problems will surely arise. Just like the farmer young folks should have a vision as to what their future should look like and carry that picture with them at all times.

Pretrial Marriage

I am certain that this topic will surely incur the raft of my extremely religious friends but before they pass judgment they should ask themselves a few questions. Inasmuch as marriages are in such shambles wouldn't it be in the best interest of the children to somehow be open to change? In the long run wouldn't it be better to try and determine if two people can live together before having three or four children and then go their separate ways due to irreconcilable differences?

If I want to move a wall and I use my head as a battering ram and said wall doesn't move an inch it would behoove me to change strategy. If I am stubborn however, I just may continue to pursue my course of action because that is the way everyone else is doing it. For the most part it really doesn't take that much prompting for an individual to convince themselves that they are correct in pursuing a certain course of action because we all from time to time think that we are smarter than everyone else.

Although we are human beings and not houses or cars, I have never purchased one without fully examining it to the best of my ability. It seems logical to me that the church should sanction some sort of premarriage agreement or arrangement wherein the couple could live together under the same roof to determine if they will be able to continue living together for the long haul. Again, I say things like this for the protection of the children which maybe born during the union.

In order for the church to avoid the appearance of being hypocritical they could stipulate in the agreement that during the pretrial period the two are not allowed or forbibben to particapte in any sexual activities. The truth of the matter is that is what it is all about anyway the couple having sex prior to marriage.

Even though the church may frown on the act of having sex before marriage how many among us in this society can actually step to the front of the line and swear that they did not have sex prior to being married so lets be for real here. Even the church must acknowledge that in many cases some people on their own opt to have pre marriages when they decide to live just together.

A great number of people decide to live together prior to getting married even though it is not sanctioned by the church. People for the most part will do exactly what they want to do. If they want to live together that is what they will do.

My point is if the church sanctioned just that aspect of living together and not the sexual aspect that would reduce some of the **stress** associated with the feeling of doing wrong. Even though all of our parents made some attempt to tell us about the birds and bees a great majority of folks still engaged in sexual activities. That is just the way it is and that is the way it will continue to be.

If two people lived together prior to being married they will know that their potential partner snores loudly at night. They will know that the person doesn' know how to correctly squeeze the tooth paste. They will learn first hand that there are too many differences to overcome. They will know whether to invest all of their hard earned money in purchasing that dream home. Which by the way will turn into a nightmare if the two are not compatible.

They will become aware of all the bills their potential partner may have which can cause financial **stress** in the long run. They will come to acquire knowledge relative to the handling of the finances. They will be able to chart their lives for the next fifty years or so not that they will adhere to said plan it is always good to have one or at least talk about one.

In most any given situation in life that is important to us as a society we have pre something. Prior to the start of the almighty football season we have pre-season games, prior to baseball, basketball, you name it. I am not just talking about sporting events. Prior to a minister getting his or her whatever they get they are required to undergo a battery of pre tests. If I want to purchase a house or car I must undergo a pre credit test in an attempt to determine if I am worthy of said credit.

Again, for the life of me or maybe because I suffer from PTSD, I cannot understand why a couple shouldn't undergo some sort of pre marriage test. Especially given the fact that we claim to care so much about our children. What better way to gauge the ability of potential mates.

Just like in the pre season of football, the appointed church member or members would be able to from time to time stop by the couple's designated living quarters and check on their progress. They would be able to give little quizzes to determine if they are prepared to go forward to the next level. The members would be able to give pointers and advise relative to formulating and keeping a sound marriage.

If I fail my pre credit check do you think for one moment that a financial institution will allow me move into an expensive house or allow me to purchase that expensive car? Again, what is more important than our children. If I fail my pre credit check and I am still interested in purchasing the home it would behoove me to take the apporpriate steps to improve my credit.

Likewise, if one of the persons fails the pre marriage test it would be required that said person find ways with the church member to improve on their score or rating so they can be married.

Sure, for the most part some of the young folks will want to continue their quest to be together regardless of what the church members may say. During the course of my life I have learned one important lesson and that is, no matter how hard one tries you can't save the world. Life is mostly about trial and error. As such, I will be the first to admit that what I am talking about may be utter nonsense to you. My point is simply this, since we know the institution of marriage is failing something needs to be done to try and save it for the sake of our children.

Is it more important in our society for us to prep ourselves for the beginning of football season rather than the preparation of our marriages which are suppose to last a life time. Strange thing about it is we relive this cycle every year. Wherein with our marriages, we just do it one time and that is just it. Let's have a marriage preseason that way we can make the necessary adjustments and if necessary a trade may just be necessary if the potential mate is not a good prospect relative to a long and enduring marriage.

As a society we seem to have no great sense of urgency relative to all of our so many failed and failing marriages. Just ensure that our sporting events are fine tuned so we can all sit back and enjoy ourselves. In the meantime, the country and our children are falling apart.

At the beginning of the regular football season each team feel that they have a sense of what their team is all about. They have a sense of knowing and recognizing their limitations. Then one day the star running back or the number one quarterback is hurt. The team at that point just doesn't throw up their hands in the air and say there goes the season. They know that they must overcome any all adversities until the end.

Like the marriage one partner can be involved in some mishap that can cause undue **stress** on the marriage. They can't or shouldn't just throw their hands in the air and say it is over especially if they have young children. What about the children?

One Must Live Their Own Life

Pardon me, but when I married you I was unaware of the fact that you were looking for a child to raise. I am truly sorry and I surely regret the fact that I led you to believe that I would walk lockstep with you in all of your endeavors whether they were right or wrong. Please forgive me for misleading you in that direction.

I will be your friend, buddy, lover or most any other thing that you may desire of me but I will never be able to abdicate all of myself to you. Moreover, even if I wanted to nature would not allow me to because I will never be able to think and discern things in the manner as you and that also applies to you.

Furthermore, we would surely lose our own personal identity and we would no longer be able to be ourselves. If you present a plan to me for the betterment of our family and if said plan appears to be sound and reasonable, I will give all of my time and attention to the project or endeavor to ensure it is implemented.

Don't get angry with me if I don't understand your plan just take the time to explain it to me. After all, I cannot see things from your mind's eye. You may be even much smarter than me but that doesn't give you the right to call me dummy just because I can't grasp your point.

When you called me dummy for not understanding your plan, you only gave me incentive to fight you instead of attempting to cooperate with you. Maybe you should start over and this time realize that I am not you and that I can only see things from my own personal perspective. If I am too slow you should have considered that and factored that into the equation prior to our marriage.

You ask me to just trust you and as you must be fully aware of, at one point in our marriage I did put all of my trust in your decision making process and it has gotten us head over heels in debt. No, I am not about to give up on you I will however be more proactive in the decisions being made around here. As they say sometimes two heads are better than one.

Even now I am not questioning your concern and care for our family because I know that you deeply care about us all and I know that you want the very best for us. Its just that sometimes in our quest to obtain what is best we may lose sight of some of the obstacles that maybe keeping us from reaching our desired objectives. I will be your second pair of eyes like a devils advocate. That will not be done with the idea of a challenge toward you but rather to give you a broader view of the overall picture.

You must understand that when we entered into this union we did so with the knowledge that we were both adults. I had no desire or intentions of treating you as a child. I can bring no more to the table than what I possess. I will never ever make an attempt to be you and hopefully you feel the same way.

We must find some neutral ground that will allow both of us to feel comfortable in our own sphere. I must allow you to be all that you can be within the confines of your own space. Just remember that in our desire to achieve that objective, the family takes precedence over any and everything that you may come up with.

If the implementation of the successful family is your number one priority, I will follow you to the very end of the universe, But don't take your frustrations out on me.

There Ought To Be A Law

I will never forget during the time when I was a teenager and wanted to obtain my driver's license. In order for me to qualify, I had to study a booklet which contained all the rules of the road. This was a safety measure enacted by every state in the union to ensure all motorist who operated a vehicle on our nation's highways was at least familiar with the rules of the road.

If a police officer stopped you for violating an established rule of the road it was not a question of whether you knew about the rule that you violated but rather, inasmuch as you possessed a driver's license you had at some point prior to the acquisition clearly shown that you fully understood the rules governing the road. The fact that you had a driver's license in your possession demonstrated that you had agreed to comply with all the established regulations.

Due to the many perils associated with operating a motor vehicle all jurisdictions enacted laws in an attempt to keep unsafe drivers off the road. They knew that in order to reduce the number of accidents on our nation's highways some of which ended in death, it would behoove them to ensure clear guidelines were put in place so each and everyone of us would clearly understands what driving is all about.

The question therefore begs are more people killed on our roads and highways or are more people killed as a result of coming from dysfunctional families? When the powers that be realized that too many folks were dying on our highways they took action to make our highways safer. We clearly see the number of crimes associated with children coming from dysfunction families. Believe it or not crimes committed by most anyone can create a desire by others even from wealthy families to copy said crimes if they think some sort of thrill can be derived from their action.

The point that I am attempting to make is the fact that inasmuch as crime can be associated with dysfunctional families why aren't the powers that be making the necessary adjustments to curtail this fact. We in this country doesn't seem to take the institution of marriage that seriously. In some parts of this country two dogs or two cats could apply for a marriage license and be granted one.

When applying for a marriage license in this country at least when I applied for one many years ago I didn't have to in anyway demonstrate that I had any knowledge or concept of what marriage was all about. There were no general questions asking me how domestic violence comes about in a family. Yet, as nearly as many people die in some form or the other from domestic violence as on our highways.

When I applied for my marriage license there were no general questions that would alert me to the many dangers associated with marriage. For example, when couple are arguing when should they take a time out and go to a neutral corner prior to the on set of domestic violence. No warning signs like on the highway.

I guess that one could argue that there are no set rules governing marriage so the government would have a very difficult time giving folks a test. I would reply by saying initially there were no set rules governing driving but as time passed it became clear that some were needed. So the powers that be assembled a group of reasonably intelligent people to make the rules governing driving especially after seeing so many people being killed.

Inasmuch as we know that the break up of a marriage is a very serious determinant to the well being of our society everything should be done to improve on that. One might even say that the only thing that the government would be able to do or say is just tell the couple to do the right thing.

Well what about bigamy? Test the couple on that. What about domestic violence (the real killer)? Test the couple on that. What about incest? Test the couple on that. What about how to establish priorities? Test them on that. What about the needs of the children? Test them on that. Those are just a few of the things that could make up a marriage test. If I who is just an average person can come up with those, I am certain that the powers that be can empower a group of professional experts and other learned scholars to come up with a standardized test that would surely benefit marriages in this country.

As we are aware the issuance of the driver's license did not stop the mayhem on our highways it did however provide a system wherein each and everyone of us are accountable for our own personal actions when we get behind the wheel of a vehicle.

Please know that I am in no way attempting to downgrade or put down the seriousness of domestic violence just trying to prove a point. It would seem that inasmuch as the powers that be didn't forewarn me about all the inherent dangers associate within a marriage they shouldn't have the authority to arrest me for violating a law that I had no knowledge of.

To that you may say that it is common knowledge to never hit another person. To that I will say we allow people everyday to hit others. We allow parents to hit children and for the most part nothing is done about it. How do you think we are induced into hitting each other in the first place. It starts with the children. A parent hits a child and somewhere in the child's brain he or she starts to reason that when a problem needs to be resolved you use force. The state itself even sanctions killing people.

I was led to believe that when two people applied for a marriage license the two of them became one. Seems to me that since I am one with the other I can do to them whatever I want because I can do unto me whatever I want. That line of thought seems to indicate that the other person becomes the other's property.

That in and of itself should prompt those in power to revisit this marriage thing. The powers that be would not just allow me to walk into my nearest motor vehicle department and explain to them that I want or need a driver's license and they just issued me one. That would not happen because they know that driving can be dangerous especially for someone who doesn't understand the rules of the road.

Doctors, lawyers, teachers, police officer, all must have some license or certificate to practice their craft. The very same standards should also apply to marriage. Why are families expected to be the backbone of the nation if they in fact are not cognizant of the rules of marriage?

How can any jurisdiction in this country have the audacity to enforce bigamy laws when it is perfectly okay to lie about all other aspects of a marriage union. If a couple is seeking a divorce, they will have lied about saying that they would stay together. Charge them with lying about that. How can the couple be seeking a divorce when they are both alive anyway? I thought they were suppose to remain together until the death of one or the other. Charge them with that. If adultery is proven charge the culprit with that.

Checklist/Application

It has always amazed me that usually whenever folks in our society talk about correcting or addressing a serious problem in this country the first words that are uttered is the financial impact said implementation will have on the economy. Yet, whenever the powers that be want to implement a law or rule that will be beneficial to themselves they will pass said law hands down. What is the financial impact for operating prisons?

Prior to the issuance of a marriage license each applicant should be required to take a test just like with the driver's license process. If the applicant is deficient in an area of the test and does not pass said applicant should not be issued a license until by becomes proficient.

Just plain crazy you might say. Well from my life's experiences, I have found that a lots of things that can help mankind started out as being some crazy idea. With the break up of so many marriages this country we should be open to any advise or suggestion that might help the situation.

I continue to talk about the marriage situation because I see a direct correlation between crime and the break up of marriages. The nonchalant manner is which we view the break up of our families that I don't care attitude. I will pay my lawyer to out lie yours and get what I want while you get little or nothing.

I have come to despise you so much that I will do everything in my power to ensure your downfall. What about the children, oh they will be alright. How can one say the children will be alright when one parent or the other is attempting to destroy the one thing that the children loves the most. Their parents.

Children for the most part will love both mom and dad even if one parent is attempting to poison the children's mind against the other. You see when a parent tells a child to hate the other, in a child's mind he or she will say I hate you but really have no concept of what they are really saying. A child may say mom or dad, I really hate you now will you please take me to McDonalds.

In the long run however, when the child is able to delineate between right and wrong the child will in fact start to actually hate the other parent. What however, the parent that is teaching the hate doesn't understand is the fact that once a child learns to hate that same hate can also be directed toward them.

As with love if love is taught the child can easily learn to love others. Both emotions are equally as strong as the other.

The two most important people that will determine whether the marriage will last will be the two participants. Given that fact, it should be mandatory that all participants who apply for a marriage license undergo a battery of test or questions to determine their knowledge of marriage.

Each participant would be given a standard form to fill out with a multitude of questions. Before the issuance of the license the participants would either have to appear before a church official or a state sponsored group who would at that time determine their eligibility status. In an attempt to get a general idea of what the form may look like, I have made and listed a mocked one.

A great number of people get married everyday without any prior knowledge of the other's background. Although to be in love may be great I am certain that you have heard the saying that love want pay the bills.

The potential partner could even be a criminal, killer or even someone from a mental institution but for the most part when we are smitten by love we never ever stop to question or look into that possible aspect of a person. All we see at that time is something that glitters like gold. It is a very sad day when the gold that we thought we saw turns out to be rust.

Putting the love aside for a moment this form will at least allow the potential partner to get somewhat of an indepth look into the individual. Like in anything else people will lie about almost anything. Given that don't stop there, have a criminal background check done. The person may be wanted by the law and after the marriage when the two of you are relaxing at home your home just may become one of those scenes that you see on those police shows.

If possible have the potential partner submit to a lie detector test. If you are going to sleep next to this person on a nightly basis you need to know if you need to sleep with one eye open.

If the potential mate has a problem with your request to obtain as much information about him or her they just may have something to hide. If we are to become partners for life we can't go around withholding secrets from each other.

Marriage Eligibility Form
(To be completed by all marriage applicants)

1. **Last Name**_____ 2. **First Name**_____

3. **DOB**_____ 4. **SSN**_____ 5. **Age**_____

6. **List Any Other Names or Alias you have ever used**_____

7. **Current Employment Status**, (if presently unemployed, move

on to the next question) working_____ where_____

how long_____ work phone number_____ salary_____

8. **Currently unemployed**, but, have qualified for a job and

waiting to be called_____ will start a new job within the next

few days_____ week_____ month_____ six months_____

9. **If you have not lived at your present address for the past ten**

years, list all pervious addresses during that ten year period

_____

_____

_____

10. **Credit Score** _____ 11. **How much debt do you owe** ___

12. **Do you have any student loans, if so, how much do you owe**

_____ 13. **Have you ever filed for bankruptcy, if so, why** __

14. **Do you have a substance abuse problem, i.e., alcohol or**

drugs _____ 15. **Other than traffic, have you ever been**

arrested, if so, what was the offense and where _____

16. **Do you have a criminal record** ___yes ___no, if so, have you

ever served time in prison___yes ___no, do you have a parole or

probation officer___yes ___no 17. **Have you been married**

before ___yes ___no, if so how many times___ are you presently

and legally divorced ___yes ___N/A 18. **Do you have any**

children ___yes ___no, if so, how many___ and how much do you

pay in child support ___ 19. **Do you believe in God** ___yes ___no

if so, do you attend church ___yes ___no 20. **Do you pay any**

spousal support payments ___yes ___no 21. **If your future**

spouse has children from a prior union, will you love them and

treat them with respect and dignity and attempt to raise them

to a respectable adulthood as if they were your own _yes _no

If I apply for a house mortgage or for a car loan and my credit score does not meet the appropriate standards I will surely be dismissed by the loan company as being a credit risk. It then therefore stands to reason that if a person's credit score is bad that person should also be rejected for a marriage license. Tell you why.

If a person has clearly demonstrated a direspect for his or her obligations in life I am talking about obligations that they entered into on their own accord what would make you think that they will be able to honor any other commitments that they make in life?

Let me explain to you what I am attempting to get at. As most anyone can tell you in a young marriage the most common issue is usually money. Especially if the young couple is just starting out.

If you will remember in my **stress** topic, I defined it as being in a condition or situation wherein the mind and body is forced to carry out a function or demand that it is not comfortable with. I talked about eliminating as many of those factor as possible. I can't think of a more **stressful** situation than the lack of needed money.

The lack of money will surely sooner or later lead to many heated arguments within the marriage. It doesn't take rocket science to conclude that arguments leads to domestic violence that sometimes leads to one partner taking the life of the other. When the deaths were happening on the highways the government took action. Well, we are at that juncture in our present day society and the government, churches or anybody needs to come up with something.

The point is the government and even some of the churches does nothing to forwarn potential marriage partners about the perils associated with marriage. By using the "**Marriage Eligibility Form,**" (hereinafter MER) the government or church if they encountered a person with a poor or bad credit rating could at least counsel the potential couple and forewarn them on some of the things to expect if a marriage is financially inept.

Moreover, if prior to the marriage each potential partner had access to the other's MER they would be able to make an intelligent decision not only about the person's credit rating but other important issues associated with a successful marriage.

In order to give the MER any bite or muscle each partner would be required to have their MER notarized and if either of them entered false information that person would be liable for a lawsuit. If you will recall former President Clinton was actually impeached from the highest office in our governmental system (although not removed from office) for lying about an affair with a woman (sorry bill, you were shafted). Why would it be to far reaching for an individual to be sued for lying about their marriage vows and commitments?

You might say that action of that nature would only serve to bog down our already burdened court system. To that I say, I would rather see the court system bogged down with matters of this nature rather than with murders and all the other associated factors relative to domestic violence.

How To Maintain A Successful Marriage

Foremost, in order to determine how to maintain a successful marriage we must clearly define and understand the meaning of the word. I am not necessarily talking about the dictionary meaning but a meaning that can be broken down to the lowest common denominator so we can all identify with it. I am not talking about the professor's meaning.

Inasmuch as we are not all professors in this society we must have a simple meaning which we can all relate to. Most educators seem to dismiss that point and seem to think that everyone should be on their level. The simple fact is most of us are not and if I fail to raise my children properly they can have a negative impact on the lives of the wealthy as well as the common man in society.

In my simple mind I will define marriage as simply being **any** two people who mutually agrees to live together in the same abode for the purpose of providing companionship to the other as they grow old together. I don't care how you slice it if we continue to breathe we will surely get old. Simply put, the consequence for being young is to grow old. I am in no way putting down being or getting old it is just a matter of fact that has to be dealt with.

It therefore seems reasonable for me to conclude that we as humans need to find someone to grow old with so our final day will be enjoyed with someone that we can relate to. In looking for a mate one should always keep that in mind.

If we as humans isn't careful we can easily be tricked by nature, rather I should say we can trick ourselves into believing that we will remain young forever. Nature didn't trick us for all we have to do is look at our elders.

Inasmuch as a long term objective has been established. We must now find a reasonable and sensible way to reach said objective.

Foremost, since I know that as a human being I am a social animal, I must find ways that will successfully allow me to live with another in a manner that will allow the both of us to enjoy the fruits of life. When I was younger I often heard older folks say about their partner "you can't live with them and you can't live without them". No truer words have been spoken.

The first thing we must do is establish parameters and a simple guideline to achieve our objective.

1. Thy should not cheat on your partner

If two people decides to get married or commit to a monogamous relationship they must come to realize that this act of betrayal is the most hurtful of all and most marriages or relationships will not recover from it. Will we be at times tempted, of course we will. Just think of Eve in the garden and forever keep in mind the consequences of her actions.

2. Fully understand the consequences of a lie

You will note that I did not say never tell your partner a lie. I must be very careful here because I do not want you to come away with the impression that it is okay to lie. The fact of the matter is we all lie in one form or the other. We lie to our children about Santa Claus, we lie to the police when stopped for speeding, we lie to ourselves about changing destructive habits that negatively impact our health, etc. etc. I could go on and on but I think you get the picture.

In life there are varying degrees associated with almost anything. For example, if a person is stopped by the police for exceeding the posted speed limit by two miles per hour you would not expect the same penalty to be imposed if the person was exceeding the limit by sixty miles per hour.

We will sometimes lie to our partner to keep them from being upset about something. The point that I am attempting to make is if you tell your partner a lie will the consequence of said lie be so devastating that it will ruin the marriage?

I really hate to get into this thing about a good lie but since we all tell lies we must face that fact head on. One might say that when we lie to the children about how they receive their gifts that is a good lie. Should a spouse ask the other if he/she has paid the mortage note and the spouse lies because he/she knows it will be paid on time but he/she just want to surprise the other with a gift. Good lie?

The consequences of the aforementioned lies will not necessarily negatively impact the union. Those type of lies can be easily explained away. Matter of fact, many humans who are very selfish will accept a so-called good lie or even a bad one if they feel the results of said lie will bring about a benefit to them. Some will even attempt to get others to lie for them if they think a benefit can be derived from it. So don't put on your self-righteous robe and pretend that you never lied. We just don't like to be lied to by others if it negatively affects us.

On the other hand, what if one partner is cheating and lies about it (the fact that the person is cheating is a lie). The person would therefore be in violation of rule number one.

3. Allow the other to maintain their own identity

Based on the prior and on-going practices associated with marriage it is easy to be tricked into the belief that when you marry you must become one. As I said earlier that will never happen because nature didn't make us that way.

If anyone in a relationship fails to acknowledge that everyone has a mind of their own said relationship will be doomed.

4. Do not judge your partner

In one respect or the other we all think that we are the smartest person on this entire earth and if everyone else would only follow our lead the world would be a much better place. If your partner cannot grasp the same things at your speed that is no reason to become upset.

5. Remain focused on the primary objective

6. Eliminate as stress as possible in the relationship

7. Keep all others including family out of your business

8. Realize that you are in a partnership

9. Realize that you are not always right

10. Learn to compromise

Epilogue

As in any writing, advice, directions or instructions, what may be good for some or even a few may not necessarily be good for all. In reading this book I am certain that you could identify with some of the things that were said while on the other hand, I am certain that you found some of the things mentioned to be totally absurd. Either way it is my contention that something must be done to save our children.

You may have found a bit of humor or you may even say that some of the ideas were just plain crazy. However, I will tell you what is not funny, domestic violence, children growing up in dysfunctional families, death and other injuries associated with domestic violence, our children commiting crimes as a result of domestic violence, etc. etc.

When I touched on affairs, I can't think of too many people who enters a marriage with the idea of having an affair. Believe it or not many affairs are started because some folks actually becomes bored with the other. You know, same ole thing day in and day out. Just like the candy, you now have it at your disposal and given that fact there is no constant need to yearn for it.

There is no great desire or passion for the candy unless you reach for it one day and it is no longer there. When that happens, you will muster up every ounce of strenght to reclaim it. If you think someone has run off with or about to run off with your candy you will vigorously use every means that you know of to get your candy back.

When and if you happen to find it you will be very attentive for a while and subsequently slip right back into that mode of taking it for granted. The cycle goes on and on.

A very good way to break the boredom cycle in a marriage is to take a brief vacation from each other. Let me explain. No, I am not talking about one partner or the other getting on a plane and jetting off to some vacation resort alone. Remember, all problems must be resolved in the home otherwise, you are opening yourself up for trouble.

I am talking about an in-house vacation from each other. Even if you have not graduated to the separate bedroom principle, take a vacation from the other by sleeping in another room for a weekend or for whatever period the two of you agree upon.

If at all possible, during the specified period avoid all contact with each other. When the two of you reunite you will be amazed at how much you really appreciate the other.

We must all come to the realization that just like the farmer, we must cultivate a relationship while the seeds are young. Otherwise, just like the old dog there will come a time that we can no longer chase the vehicle. We too will become so old that even if we see something worth chasing, we will be so old that the only thing that we will be able to do is lift our heads and just think of younger days.

978-0-595-39941-3
0-595-39941-X

Printed in the United States
135368LV00008BA/53/A

9 780595 399413